Meet Your Happy Chemicals

Loretta Graziano Breuning, PhD

Meet Your Happy Chemicals

Dopamine, Endorphin, Oxytocin, Serotonin

Loretta Graziano Breuning, PhD

Inner Mammal Institute

copyright 2012
by Loretta Graziano Breuning
Inner Mammal Institute
all rights reserved
fourth edition
ISBN- 978-1-941959-01-5

contact: Loretta@innermammalinstitute.org
www.innermammalinstitute.org

also by Loretta G. Breuning, PhD

Beyond Cynical
Transcend Your Mammalian Negativity

I, Mammal
Why Your Brain Links Status and Happiness

Your Neurochemical Self
PsychologyToday.com blog

Inner Mammal Institute

Human moods and motivations are caused by brain chemicals inherited from earlier animals. These chemicals evolved to promote survival, not to make you happy all the time. You can stimulate more of the happy chemicals when you know how they work in the state of nature. The Inner Mammal Institute offers books, free resources, and coaching options that can help. Transcend the disease-based view of the brain and embrace the nature in human nature. Sign up for the monthly newsletter, **Private Lives of Primates**, at:
www.innermammalinstitute.org

for my
wonderful
husband, Bill

Table of Contents

Introduction

Happy Chemicals Turn Off So They Can Turn On

The feeling we call "happiness" comes from four special brain chemicals: *dopamine, endorphin, oxytocin* and *serotonin*. These "happy chemicals" spurt when your brain sees something good for your survival. Then they turn off, so they're ready to spurt again when something good crosses your path.

Each happy chemical triggers a different good feeling. Dopamine produces the joy of finding what you seek- the "Eureka! I got it!" feeling. Endorphin produces the oblivion that masks pain- often called "euphoria." Oxytocin produces the feeling of being safe with others- now called "bonding." And serotonin produces the feeling of being respected by others-"pride."

"I don't see happiness this way," you may say. You don't think this in words because neurochemicals work without words. But you can easily see these motivations in your fellow man. And research shows that animals have these same basic neurochemicals doing the same basic jobs. As for yourself, it's easy to believe that your verbal inner voice is your whole thought process, and ignore your neurochemical self.

Happy chemicals are controlled by tiny brain structures that all mammals have in common: the hippocampus, amygdala, pituitary, hypothalamus, and other parts collectively known as the **limbic system.** In humans, the limbic system is surrounded by a huge cortex. These two different brain systems are always working together, trying to keep you alive and keep your DNA alive. Each has its special job. Your cortex looks for patterns in the present that match patterns you stored in the past. Your limbic system releases neurochemicals that tell your body *"this is good for you, go toward it,"* and *"this is bad for you, avoid it."* Your body doesn't always act on these messages because your cortex can override them. Then, your limbic system tries again. The cortex can over-ride the limbic system momentarily, but your mammal brain is the core of who you are.

Four happy chemicals	
dopamine	the joy of finding what you seek
endorphin	the oblivion that masks pain
oxytocin	the safety of social bonds
serotonin	the security of social dominance

© 2012 L. Breuning

Your brain rewards you with good feelings when you do something good for your survival. Each of the happy chemicals motivates a different type of survival behavior. Dopamine motivates you to get what you need, even when it takes lots of effort. Endorphin motivates you to ignore pain so you can escape from harm when you're injured. Oxytocin motivates you to trust others, to find safety in companionship. And serotonin motivates you to get respect, which expands your mating opportunities and protects your offspring.

Happy survival motives	
dopamine	keep seeking rewards
endorphin	ignore physical pain
oxytocin	build social alliances
serotonin	get respect from others

© 2012 L. Breuning

The mammal brain motivates a body to go toward things that trigger happy chemicals, and avoid things that trigger unhappy chemicals. You can restrain yourself from acting on a neurochemical impulse, but then your brain generates another impulse. You are always using neurochemicals to decide what is good for you and what to avoid. Your cortex helps by directing attention and sifting information, but your limbic brain sparks the action.

We struggle to make sense of our neurochemical ups and downs because they don't come from verbal logic. They come from the operating system we've inherited from our ancestors. Once you know how the mammal brain works, your neurochemical ups and downs are easier to accept.

Happy chemicals did not evolve to be on all the time. They evolved to promote your survival. It may not seem that way because the mammal brain defines survival its own way. It relies on early experience, even though children can't understand survival realistically. And it cares as much for the survival of your genes as it does for your body.

This quirky brain complicates the business of being human. We have no choice but to work with the brain we've got. If you know how it works, you can get more happy chemicals from it, and avoid more unhappy chemicals.

It's foolish to think of your cortex as the good guy and your limbic system as the bad guy. You need both to make sense of the world around you. Your cortex sees the world as a chaos of raw detail until your limbic system labels things as good for you or bad for you. More important, your cortex cannot produce happy chemicals. If you want to be happy, you have to get it from your limbic system.

But your cortex and your limbic system are literally not on speaking terms. That's because the limbic system can't process language. When you talk to yourself, it's all in your cortex. The limbic system never tells you in words why it is spurting a happy or unhappy chemical. Animals accept their neurochemical impulses without expecting a verbal rationale. That's why animals can help us make sense of our own brain chemicals. The goal here is not to glorify animals or primitive impulses. The goal is to understand our neurochemical ups and downs.

Comparing brain parts

cortex	extra neurons that store life experience by growing and interconnecting
limbic system	structures that manage neuro-chemicals, such as the amygdala, hippocampus, hypothalamus
reptilian brain	the cerebellum and brain stem (medulla oblongata and pons), which manage routine bodily functions
human	
chimpanzee	
gazelle	
mouse	
lizard	

A hungry lion is happy when he sees prey.[1] It's not philosophical happiness. His happy chemicals cause a state of arousal that releases energy for the hunt. Lions often fail in their hunts, and they choose their targets carefully to avoid running out of energy before they get to eat. So a lion is thrilled when he sees a gazelle close at hand. His dopamine surges, which revs up his motor to pounce.

A thirsty elephant is happy when he finds water. The good feeling of quenching his thirst triggers dopamine, which makes permanent connections in his neurons. That helps him find water again in the future. He need not "try" to learn where water is. Dopamine simply paves a neural pathway. The next time he sees any sign of a water hole, electricity zips down the path to his happy chemicals. The good feeling tells him "here is what you need." Without effort or intent, happy chemicals promote survival.

But happy chemicals don't flow constantly. The lion only gets more happy chemicals when he finds more prey, and the elephant only spurts when he meets a survival need. In nature, there is no free happy chemical. Good feelings evolved because they get us to keep doing things that promote survival.

Your Happy Trails

Your feelings are unique. You have unique ways to turn on your happy chemicals because you built neural pathways from your unique life experience. When something made you feel good as a child, the happy chemicals built connections.

---

[1] I use the male pronoun in this book because it combines with my female voice to convey the universal aspects of brain function. Female lions do most of the hunting, in fact, but gender differences are widely expounded elsewhere. This book focuses on the physiology that both genders have in common.

When something felt bad, your unhappy chemicals seared that information, too. Over time, some of your neural pathways developed into superhighways because you activated them a lot. The survival system you ended up with is not what you'd design today if you started from scratch. It's the survival system that emerged from real experience.

Your existing neural highway system makes it easy for you to like some things and dislike other things. Often, we find ourselves liking things that are not especially good for us, and fearing things that are good for us. Why would a brain that evolved for survival build such quirky pathways?

Because the brain builds on the pathways it already has. We evolved to store experience, not to delete it. Most of the time, experience holds important lessons. It helps us go toward things that helped us in the past and avoid things that endangered us. But a huge surge of happy chemical builds a huge pathway, even if too much of a good thing can hurt you. A big surge of unhappy chemical builds a big circuit that lasts even when the threat is gone. This promotes survival in a world where good things are scarce, and threats are enduring. Your brain relies on its pathways as if your life depended on it because in the state of nature, it does.

You built circuits effortlessly when you were young. Building new circuits in adulthood is like trying to slash a new trail through dense rainforest. Every step requires a huge effort, and the new trail disappears into the undergrowth if you don't use it again soon. Such trail-blazing feels inefficient and downright unsafe when a nice superhighway is nearby. That's why people tend to stick with the pathways they have.

You can build new trails through your jungle of neurons, which can turn on your happy chemicals in new ways. It's harder than you'd expect, but it's easier when you know your equipment.

The electricity in your brain flows like water. It finds the path of least resistance. Electricity doesn't flow easily along neurons you've never activated before. Each time a neural pathway is activated, electricity flows more easily. Repetition develops a neural trail slowly, the way a dirt path hardens from years of use. But neurochemicals develop a neural trail instantly, the way asphalt paves a dirt road. Your neural network grew from things you experienced repeatedly and things you experience neurochemically.

Once you've built highways to your happy chemicals, you use them, because it feels like you're promoting survival. New highways are hard to build in later life. You can always add new leaves to your neural branches, but it's harder to add new roots. It's possible, but it doesn't happen in the effortless way it did in youth. You have to spend a lot of time choosing the experiences you feed to your brain. No one can build new pathways for you, and you cannot build them for someone else. But this book will help by showing just what stimulates happy chemicals and what connects neurons. It can be your guide as you work to slash new roads and avoid old ones.

This brain we've inherited is frustrating. In its quest for survival, it often turns unhappy chemicals on and happy chemicals off. When my neurochemistry frustrates me, I remind myself that it has succeeded at promoting survival for millions of years.

The Vicious Cycle of Happy Chemicals

When your unhappy chemicals flow, you don't usually respond by thanking them for promoting your survival. Instead, you focus on ways to trigger happy chemicals. For example, when hunger triggers a bad feeling, a mammal seeks food. When cold triggers a bad feeling, a mammal seeks warmth. Just finding food and warmth triggers happy chemicals, before you actually eat or warm up. Happy chemicals flow when you see a way to meet your needs.

The human cortex is good at avoiding bad feelings. We avoid hunger and chill by planting food and stocking fuel. But unhappy chemicals remain, no matter how well we meet our needs. As soon as you're warm and fed, your brain scan for other things that can hurt you. Your survival is threatened as long as you're alive, and your brain never stops looking for survival threats.

A mammal must take risks to get its needs met. It risks getting killed by a predator while foraging for food. It risks social conflict when seeking mates. It risks losing its offspring before grandchildren have been produced to preserve its genes. Unhappy chemicals are the brain's way of alerting us to such risks.

Unhappy chemicals feel bad because that works. It gets your attention, fast. It's comforting to know that bad feelings have a purpose. When a hungry gazelle smells a lion, bad feelings motivate it to run rather than keep eating. The gazelle survives because the smell of a lion triggers a feeling that's much worse than ordinary hunger. Once the gazelle escapes from the lion, the bad feeling of hunger gets its attention again, and it looks for a safe place to forage. We are alive today because unhappy chemicals got our ancestors' attention to one survival threat after another.

Bad feelings are produced by *cortisol*. Your response to cortisol depends on what it's paired with, be it low blood sugar, the scent of a predator, social exclusion, or myriad other danger signals. When your cortisol flows, it links the neurons active in your brain at that moment. This wires you to recognize those danger cues in the future. A young gazelle has cortisol spurts while following its mother, and the pathways it builds prepare it to survive when its mother is gone. Survival knowledge builds without effort or intent because neurochemicals pave pathways.

When you feel a cortisol alert, your brain looks for a way to make it stop. Sometimes the solution is obvious, like pulling your hand off a hot stove. But bad feelings don't always have obvious causes. And they don't always have obvious cures. Such feelings keep commanding your attention with the sense that you must "do something." Your brain keeps scanning the world for a way to make bad feelings stop.

That "do something" feeling promotes survival, but it also causes trouble. It motivates us to do anything that stops the cortisol. Can eating a donut fix a career or romantic setback? From your brain's perspective, it can. Consciously, you know the donut doesn't solve the problem. But when something changes unhappy chemicals to happy chemicals, your brain learns from the experience. When donuts trigger happy chemicals (because fat and sugar are scarce in nature), a neural pathway is paved. The next time you have that "do something" feeling, this pathway is one "something" you "know." You may not act on it, because you also know the consequences, and you've built other "do something" pathways. But it remains in your mammal brain's arsenal of survival strategies.

Cortisol is triggered by disappointment. Your mammal brain alerts you when your expectations are not met. That "do something!" feeling gets your attention as long as expectations of romance or success are disappointed, and your brain responds with the strategies it has learned.

We evolved to learn from experience. It might seem that people don't learn from experience until you look at it neurochemically. Neurochemicals are molecules that make physical changes in the brain. These changes help you navigate through the world by triggering good or bad feelings when something felt good or bad in your past. This promotes survival when things that trigger good feelings are indeed good for survival. And when these feelings are bad for survival, we can "second guess" our neurochemical steering mechanism with our big cortex. That's what the cortex evolved for. But it can't work alone. It is always working along with our neurochemistry.

Each brain has a network of connections built from experiences that felt good in the past. These connections represent simple things like donuts and complex things like social trust and practical skills. By the time you are old enough to choose your own course of action, you already have a brain full of circuits that turn your neurochemicals on and off. These circuits are what you "know" about how to survive in the world. You can stop yourself from acting on your neurochemical impulses, which gives your brain time to search for a Plan B. But you are always relying on your existing pathways to plot a course that leads away from cortisol and toward happy chemicals.

When you succeed at triggering happy chemicals, the spurt is soon over. To get more, you have to do more. That is how a brain keeps prodding a body to do what it takes to keep its DNA alive. Happy chemicals get re-absorbed and your awareness of survival threats resumes. You get that "do something" feeling, and you ponder your options by sending electricity down the pathways you have.

The brain's quest for happy chemicals often leads to a vicious cycle because of the side effects. "Everything I like is illegal, immoral or fattening," goes the old saying. Happy chemicals exist because of their side effects, thanks to natural selection. When happy chemicals dip and we seek more, we get more side effects. They can accumulate to the point where they trigger unhappy chemicals. Now, the behavior you use to trigger happiness creates more unhappiness. And the more cortisol you produce, the more motivated you are to repeat the behavior you expect to make you happy. You are wired for frustration.

Vicious cycles are everywhere. Some of the most familiar ones are alcohol, junk food, compulsive spending, and drugs. Other well-known vicious cycles are risk-taking, getting angry, falling in love, and rescuing others. Each of these behaviors can make you feel good in a moment when you were feeling bad. The good feeling means happy chemicals are building connections, making it easier to trigger good feelings in that way in the future. Over time, a neural superhighway develops. Now your brain activates that behavior effortlessly. But too much of a good thing triggers unhappy chemicals, which let you know that it's time to stop. It's hard to stop, however, because your brain seeks happy chemicals. So the same behavior can trigger both happy and unhappy feelings at once, like driving with one foot on the accelerator and one on the brake.

You can stop this vicious cycle in one instant. Just resist that "do something" feeling and live with the cortisol. This is not easy because cortisol screams for your attention. It did not evolve for you to sit around and accept it. But you can build the skill of doing nothing during a cortisol alert, despite that urge to make it go away in any way possible. That frees you to activate an alternative happy circuit instead of the old-familiar one. A virtuous circle starts in that moment.

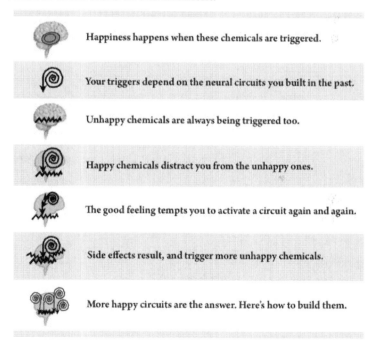

Happiness happens when these chemicals are triggered.

Your triggers depend on the neural circuits you built in the past.

Unhappy chemicals are always being triggered too.

Happy chemicals distract you from the unhappy ones.

The good feeling tempts you to activate a circuit again and again.

Side effects result, and trigger more unhappy chemicals.

More happy circuits are the answer. Here's how to build them.

But what if you don't have an alternative circuit at the ready? That's where this book comes in. It shows how new highways to your happy chemicals can be built. That may feel awkward because we rely so heavily on circuits that built themselves. We've all built circuits with conscious effort, like the ones that do long division and define vocabulary words. But the circuits that tell you what's good and bad for you are built from lived experience. You have to feed your brain new experiences for it to learn new ways of feeling good. And you have to keep doing it until the new circuit is big enough to compete with the ones you've already built by accident.

We think it should be easy to build new circuits since our old ones got there without struggle. This book shows why it's so hard to remodel your neural infrastructure.

Your brain likes your old circuits, even when they lead you astray. That's because electricity zipping down a well-worn pathway gives you the feeling that you know what's going on. When you refuse to use your old pathways, you may feel lost. You may even feel like you're threatening your own survival, though you're doing precisely the opposite.

The bad feeling of resisting a habit eases once a new habit forms. You can do that in 45 days. If you repeat a new thought or behavior every day without fail, in 45 days a new pathway will invite electricity away from the old path. The new choice will not make you happy on Day 1, and it may not make you happy on Day 40. Even on Day 45, your new circuit cannot trigger happy chemicals constantly. But it can trigger enough to free you from a vicious cycle. On Day 46, you'll be ready to start building another new circuit. Over time, you can build many new ways to trigger happy chemicals, as long as you're willing to repeat a behavior for 45 days even if it doesn't feel good.

A vicious cycle is easy to see in someone else. That's why people are often tempted to take charge of other people's happiness, even while doing nothing about a vicious cycle of their own. But each person must manage their own limbic system. No one else can reach into your brain and trigger your happy chemicals for you. Only you can make connections in your brain, and you cannot make connections in someone else's brain. If you focus your life on other people's brains, you may fail to fix their vicious cycles and your own.

Modern society is not the cause of vicious cycles. Our ancestors had their own variations. They felt good when they made human sacrifices, and when the good feeling passed they made more sacrifices. Over time, humans developed better ways to trigger happy chemicals and avert unhappy chemicals.

It's not easy being a mammal with a big cortex. We have enough neurons to imagine things that don't exist instead of just focusing on what is. This allows us to improve things, but it also leaves us feeling that something is wrong with the world as it is. A vicious cycle often results. The more you make yourself happy by imagining a "better world," the less invested you are in the world as it is. This can lead to bad decisions that trigger unhappy chemicals, motivating you to live in your imagined world even more. Reality is a disappointment compared to the ideal world that a cortex can imagine.

What About Love?

You've probably heard that loving others is the key to happiness. It's a good principle, but it only provides limited insight into your happy chemicals.

Love triggers huge neurochemical ups and downs because it plays a huge role in the survival of your genes. Our brain uses happy chemicals to reward behaviors that promote what biologists call "reproductive success." You may not care about reproducing and you surely have another definition for success. You may feel sure that your love is selfless and completely unconcerned with your genes. But you are here today because your ancestors successfully competed for mates and kept their offspring alive long enough to successfully mate. Your limbic system was naturally selected over millions of years for its ability to reproduce. As soon as a mammal is safe from immediate harm, its thoughts turn to reproductive success in all of its aspects.

Sex and romance are just the obvious examples. Nurturing children promotes your genes, so it's not surprising that it stimulates happy chemicals. Competing successfully for quality mates promotes your genes, and it stimulates happy chemicals. Over the millennia, some DNA made a lot of copies of itself and some made none at all. A conscious intent to reproduce is not necessary for neurochemicals to motivate behavior. For example, animals avoid in-breeding. They don't do that consciously, but natural selection weeded out in-breeders, leaving brains that produced alternative behaviors to flourish. Our brains are inherited from the flourishers.

Unhappy chemicals promote reproductive success too. In nature, females often watch their offspring get eaten alive by predators, and males suffer conflict and rejection in their quest for mates. The bad feeling of cortisol motivates an animal to do what it takes to avoid threats and trigger happy chemicals. Bad feelings motivate a mother mammal to guard her child constantly, and search for the nourishment she needs to sustain her milk. Bad feelings motivate a male mammal to avoid conflicts he's likely to lose, and risk conflicts he's likely to win.

Social alliances promote reproductive success in the state of nature. Mammals with more social allies and more status in their social group tend to have more surviving offspring. Natural selection produced a brain good at social skills as a result. The mammal brain promotes social success by rewarding it with happy chemicals. And if your social standing is threatened, the mammal brain warns you with cortisol because it's a threat to your DNA in the state of nature.

Each happy chemical rewards love in a different way. When you know how each one is linked to reproductive success, the frustrations of life make sense.

Dopamine is stimulated by the "chase" aspect of love. It's also triggered when a baby hears his mother's footsteps. Dopamine alerts us that our needs are about to be met. Female chimpanzees are known to be partial to males who share their meat after a hunt. Female reproduction depends heavily on protein, which is very scarce in the rainforest, so opportunities to meet this need trigger lots of dopamine. For humans, finding "the one" makes you high on dopamine because a longer quest to meet a need stimulates a longer surge.

Oxytocin is stimulated by touch, and by social trust. In animals, touch and trust go together. Apes only allow trusted companions to touch them because they know from experience that violence can erupt in an instant. In humans, oxytocin is stimulated by everything from holding hands to feeling supported to orgasm. Holding hands stimulates a small amount of oxytocin, but when repeated over time, as in the case of an elderly couple, it builds up a circuit that easily triggers social trust. Sex triggers a lot of oxytocin at once, yielding lots of social trust for a very short time. Childbirth triggers a huge oxytocin spurt, both in mother and child. Nurturing other people's children can stimulate it too, as can nurturing adults, depending on the circuits one has built. Friendship bonds stimulate oxytocin, and in the monkey and ape world, research shows that individuals with more social alliances have more reproductive success.

Serotonin is stimulated by the status aspect of love– the pride of associating with a person of a certain stature. You may not think of your own love in this way, but you can easily see it in others. Animals with higher status in their social groups have more "reproductive success," and natural selection created a brain that seeks status by rewarding it with serotonin. This may be hard to believe, but research on huge range of species shows tremendous energy invested in the pursuit of status. Social dominance leads to more mating opportunity and more surviving offspring– and it feels good. We no longer try to survive by having as many offspring as possible, but when you receive the affection of a desirable individual, it triggers lots of serotonin, though you hate to admit it. And when you are the desired individual, receiving admiration from others, that triggers serotonin too. It feels so good that people tend to seek it again and again.

Endorphin is stimulated by physical pain. Crying also stimulates endorphin. If a loved one causes you pain, the endorphin that's released paves neural pathways, wiring you to expect a good feeling from pain in the future. People may tolerate painful relationships because their brain learned to associate it with the good feeling of endorphin. Confusing love and pain is obviously a bad survival strategy. Roller-coaster relationships are easier to transcend when you understand endorphin.

The sex hormones, like testosterone and estrogen, are central to the feelings we associate with love. They are outside the scope of this book, however, because they do not trigger the feeling of happiness. They mediate specific physical responses instead.

Why did the brain evolve so many different ways to motivate reproductive behavior? Because keeping your DNA alive is harder than you'd think. Survival rates are low in the state of nature, and mating opportunities are harder to come by than you might expect. Your genes got wiped off the face of the earth unless you made a serious effort. Of course, animals don't consciously intend to promote their genes. But every creature alive today has inherited the brain of ancestors who did what it took to reproduce.

There is no free love in nature. Every species has a preliminary qualifying event before mating behavior. Creatures work hard for any mating opportunity that comes their way. In the end, some DNA makes lots of copies of itself, while other DNA disappears without a trace. You may say you don't care about your DNA, but you've inherited a limbic system that does.

Unhappy chemicals creep into your life as you seek love in all its forms. Animal brains release cortisol when their social overtures are disappointed. The bad feeling motivates the brain to "do something." It reminds you that your genes will be annihilated if you don't get busy. You don't need to tell yourself that in words. Natural selection created neurochemicals that give you the message non-verbally.

Losing love triggers a huge surge of unhappy chemical. That actually promotes genetic survival because the pain you associate with the old attachment leaves you available for a new attachment. The brain has trouble ending attachments because the oxytocin pathway is still there. But if you can't break an attachment, your genes are doomed. The pain of lost love re-wires your brain so you can move on. Cortisol promotes love by helping you avoid places where you're not getting it.

Love often disappoints for a subtle reason that's widely overlooked. A young child learns to expect others to meet their needs. Children cannot meet their own needs, so love equals survival to the young brain. Eventually you have to start meeting your own needs. When the expectation of being cared for is disappointed, it can feel like a survival threat. Childhood is a luxury evolved by mammals, but it comes with a painful transition from dependence to independence. Lots of cortisol is triggered as you learn that you cannot trust the world to meet your needs for you. This independence is natural, for a species can only survive if each generation learns to meet its needs without its parents. And if you had parents who were not trustworthy in the first place, you had more cortisol, sooner. The sense of disappointment and loss motivates people to let go of childhood expectations and find love in adult ways. And that keeps our genes alive.

When disappointment in love gives you that bad cortisol feeling, your brain looks for ways to trigger good feelings. There are limitless ways to do that. Sometimes a person seeks a new mating partner, and sometimes a person focuses on nurturing children. Sometimes a person tries to contribute to mankind at large and sometimes a person uses violence to hold onto their "loved" ones. These behaviors seem very different, but they are all motivated by the expectation of happy chemicals. Expectations depend on the circuits each individual has built from life experience.

In modern times, many people expect romantic love to be part of their life all the time. Expectations were different in the past. Sex created children, and if you lived to middle age, you could expect to be surrounded by grandchildren. But people had the same basic neurochemistry. No matter how you learn to trigger happy chemicals, each burst lasts for a short time and you have to do more to get more. Maybe that's why love songs are always popular. They activate neurochemicals with fewer messy side effects.

Love triggers a cocktail of neurochemicals because it's so highly relevant to survival. But it cannot guarantee non-stop happiness. It feels like it can while you're enjoying the cocktail, however, so your brain may learn to expect that.

The Chapters Ahead

Chapter 1 describes the distinct feeling of each happy chemical. We'll see how dopamine, endorphin, oxytocin, and serotonin evolved to reward specific survival behaviors. And we'll see how rewards create expectations about future rewards.

Chapter 2 explores unhappy chemicals. They get our attention when we face threats. Unhappiness will always be with us because a big-brained social animal can always find potential threats to its prospects. The chapter presents an array of threats that alarm your limbic system without your intellect knowing why.

Chapter 3 shows how disappointment leads to a vicious cycle. Disappointment is inevitable because happy chemicals evolved to alert you to *new* survival information. The same old happy-chemical stimulators don't give you the happiness you expect after a while. But you keep expecting because the pathway is still there. If you respond by repeating the behavior over and over, side effects accumulate. The chapter describes dopamine disappointment, endorphin disappointment, oxytocin disappointment, and serotonin disappointment. The vicious cycle can stop if you build new happy circuits.

Chapter 4 shows how neural circuits develop. Life experience makes permanent physical changes in brain cells. We'll look at five kinds of physical changes, and why they occur more easily in youth. We'll see how repetition and emotion control learning, including social learning.

Chapter 5 presents strategies for building new happy circuits. Repeating a brief thought or action each day for 45 days builds a new superhighway, which relieves dependence on an old vicious cycle. Alternatives for dopamine happiness, endorphin happiness, oxytocin happiness, and serotonin happiness are suggested as a starting point.

Why do people choose to be unhappy rather than build new happy circuits? Chapter 6 explores common thought habits, such as: "I shouldn't have to do that." "It sounds selfish." "I can't lower my standards." "The system has to change first." "I won't be able to do it." Those who refuse to take responsibility for their own happy chemicals often try to make themselves responsible for other people's happy chemicals, and expect others to be responsible for theirs. The chapter explains why this strategy fails.

Chapter 7 addresses the burden of choice. We all have free will because we can use our pre-frontal cortex to inhibit our neurochemical impulses. You can make choices that increase your happiness, but it doesn't happen automatically. It requires a constant weighing of trade-offs between the potential rewards of one course of action and another. We can never predict the outcome of our actions with certainty. This exposes us to uncertainty, disappointment, frustration, and cortisol. Choice brings a huge potential for unhappy chemicals. Since the brain strives to avoid unhappy chemicals, people find ways to avoid choice. One way of doing that is to imagine "a better world" that supplies happiness constantly and eliminates unhappiness. It feels good to imagine your happiness guaranteed, without the pressure of difficult trade-offs. It feels bad to see how the real world falls short of your ideal world. But if you seek happiness by living in an imagined world, you leave your real-world choices to others. The result is disappointment and another vicious cycle. Chapter 7 shows how to break it by accepting the trade-offs and uncertainties inherent in free choice.

The Author's Note at the end of the book provides background about my personal quest for happy chemicals. The Source Note that follows explains why this book is not foot-noted. At the end is a collection of postcards displaying the book's core ideas. Color downloads of these postcards are available at no charge at meetyourhappychemicals.com.

And now let's meet the happy chemicals.

1
Meet Your Happy Chemicals

Your feelings are unique, but the molecules that cause your feelings are the same as everyone else's.

Your life experience is unique, but it overlaps with others because each brain focuses on its own survival.

You may not think you're focused on your own survival. Your aim is loftier when you talk to yourself in words. But your happy chemicals respond to improvements in your survival prospects, however you've learned to define them.

Meet Your Dopamine

A marathon runner gets a surge of dopamine when he sees the finish line. A football player is fueled by dopamine as he scores and does a victory dance. "I did it!" the brain tells the body. It feels so good that the brain looks for ways to trigger the feeling again.

Of course, dopamine didn't evolve for crossing arbitrary lines on the ground. It evolved to release energy when you're about to meet a survival need. If an ape climbs a high tree for a delicious mango, dopamine spurts as he nears the reward. That tells his body to release the reserve tank of energy, which helps him do what it takes to meet his needs. He doesn't say "I did it!" in words, but neurochemicals create that feeling without need for words.

When that ape was young, a bite of mango triggered his dopamine because it's full of survival-enhancing sugar. That paved a circuit which now spurts dopamine as soon as he sees a way to get another mango.

Dopamine helped our ancestors survive by managing their energy. They foraged for food by walking slowly until they saw something that looked promising. That triggered dopamine, and they surged ahead. The mammal brain scans constantly for potential rewards, and dopamine is the signal that it has found some.

Our distant ancestors didn't know where their next meal was coming from. Humans foraged constantly before they learned to store food. They survived by scanning for evidence of food and releasing their energy when something looked promising. Evidence of a reward triggers dopamine, which motivates your body to invest its energy. Even if you are not foraging in the wilderness, you are constantly deciding when it's worth making an effort and when it's better to conserve your effort. Your dopamine circuits guide that decision.

You built those circuits from past dopamine experiences. Imagine a child foraging with his mother. The child sees her get excited when they find a delicious berry patch. Before the child ever tastes a berry, his mother's excitement activates his mirror neurons and he starts triggering dopamine. Then he tastes the berry. Such intense sweetness and flavor are rare in the state of nature, so his neurochemicals tell him "Wow! This meets your needs. Get more of it!" The dopamine surge connects all the neurons active in his brain at that moment. Those connections enable the child to find berries in the future.

The happy chemical does double duty. It creates a good feeling by unleashing energy, and it stores information that can lead you to the good feeling again. Without effort or intent, dopamine surges build a neural template that responds when you see signs of a reward you've already experienced.

Humans are not born with circuits for finding food the way most animals are. We must build these from experience. Today, we learn to forage for career opportunities, and then we might forage in a cookbook or on the Food Network. But before there were words or maps, people found food because dopamine connected neurons. When something felt good, that feeling wired you to recognize the signs when you seek more of it. Dopamine supplies the road map and the motivation to travel it.

When you taste a berry, you may not get that "Wow!" because the taste is no longer rare. Your brain saves your energy for rewards that are scarce in your life experience. When the first cherries of the season appear, I get a rush of excitement just from looking at them. But my excitement doesn't last. I can't be happy all the time by looking at cherries. My dopamine responds to things more relevant to my survival instead of wasting my energy on things that are easily available.

Social rewards can't be mass produced like sugar and berry flavoring. When you seek and find social rewards, dopamine releases energy. People invest years of effort trying to become a heart surgeon or a rock star because each step along the way triggers dopamine. Even if your goal is committing the perfect crime or living on the beach, your brain releases dopamine as you seek and find markers along the way. Which social rewards trigger your dopamine depends on the experiences that built your circuits.

Every squirt of dopamine ends, alas, and you only get more when your brain sees another chance to approach a reward.

The fleetingness of dopamine was illuminated by a recent monkey study. The animals were trained to do a task and get rewarded with spinach. After a few days, they were rewarded with squirts of juice instead of spinach. The monkeys' dopamine soared. That seared the information: "This reeeally meets your needs" into their neurons.

The experimenters continued giving the monkeys juice, and in a few days something curious happened. No dopamine spike. The monkeys' brains stopped reacting to rewards that just came on their own. In human terms, they took it for granted.

When there's no new information, there's no need for dopamine. When you need to record new survival rewards or new ways of getting them, your dopamine is there.

This experiment has a dramatic finale. The experimenters switched back to spinach, and the monkeys reacted with fits of rage. They screamed and threw the spinach back at the researchers. They had learned to expect juice, and even though it no longer made them happy, losing it made them mad.

Such research improves our understanding of dopamine significantly. For most of human history, people functioned without scientific knowledge of their neurochemistry. Then in the 1950s, an electrode was inserted into a rat's brain in a spot later held to be its dopamine or reward center. The rat could press a lever that activated the electrode. He seized the day, pushing the lever constantly until he dropped dead. He would not stop for food or water or attractive mates. At the time, scientists speculated that the electrode was in his "pleasure center." But why would a brain define pleasure in a way that motivated it to die rather than eat, drink or mate? Many decades of research later, we realize that it's the *expectation* of reward that triggers dopamine. The unfortunate rat kept expecting to get food from the lever because it triggered so much more dopamine than food itself.

Cocaine stimulates more dopamine than normal life. It gives you the thrill of finding berries or finishing a marathon without leaving the couch. You get the excitement of accomplishment without having to accomplish anything.

Mothers have been seen lifting cars when their child is pinned underneath. A huge potential reward triggers a huge surge of dopamine. Saving your child's life is the biggest reward there is from the perspective of your genes. A mother is not consciously thinking of her genes when she risks her life to save her child. She's not thinking at all. Such mothers report they had no idea what they were doing. The verbal part of the brain is not needed for a dopamine circuit to unleash the energy needed to do the job.

The link between dopamine and survival is not always obvious. For example, computer games stimulate dopamine, though they don't meet real needs. Computer games reward you with points that your mind may link to social rewards. You get the points by activating the seek-and-find mechanism that evolved for foraging. Dopamine surges each time you get the reward you seek. If a computer game gave you a good feeling at a time when you were feeling bad, your brain learns that it's a way to make bad feelings go away. Gaming eliminates survival threats, from the mammal brain's perspective. The next time you feel bad, scoring points on a computer game is one way your brain knows to feel good.

Dopamine experiences	
List examples of the joy of seeking and finding: at work, at play, in yourself and others.	

© 2012 L. Breuning

Your ancestors never stopped seeking. When their bellies were full, they looked for ways to make better arrows and better shelters. They searched for days to find the right materials. It felt good because they anticipated rewards. When they found what they sought it felt good for a moment, and then they went back to seeking. The urge for more did not start with "our society." Life experience teaches you which ways of investing your effort are likely to be rewarded, whether a material reward, a social reward, or the relief of a bad feeling.

If you are studying for a math test, you are fueled by dopamine. You may or may not consider it a "good feeling." But something in your life experience has connected math skills to other rewards. It could be material rewards, or social rewards, or just the good feeling of getting the right answer. Solving math problems is a seek-and-find activity, even though it's different from foraging. When you find that your answer is correct, you get that "I did it!" feeling, which erases any bad cortisol feelings for that moment. And if your answer is wrong, you may seek the right answer again because you still expect the reward.

Sometimes the reward you expect is another neurochemical. For example, if you expect a hug after washing the dishes, dopamine motivates you to do what it takes to get that oxytocin. If you expect a promotion after working overtime, dopamine keeps you going in expectation of the serotonin.

An athlete spends long hours training in expectation of future rewards. Each small step toward the reward triggers a small amount of dopamine. Scoring points or winning a medal triggers a big burst of dopamine. But trophies and medals are not the reward itself. They are simply evidence that the reward is approaching. An athlete expects more survival-relevant rewards, be it material rewards, or social rewards, or internal rewards, depending on the circuits that athlete has built. Dopamine tells you when to expect a reward, and you invest effort in anticipation of it. The bigger the reward and the closer you get to it, the more of that great dopamine feeling your brain releases.

Meet Your Endorphin

"Euphoria" is the word often used to describe the endorphin feeling. But this neurochemical did not evolve for good times. Physical pain is what triggers endorphin. You may have experienced this if you took a bad fall and got up thinking you were fine, only to find yourself in pain a little later.

Endorphin masks pain for a short time, which promotes survival by giving an injured mammal a chance to reach safety. If your ancestor broke his leg while hunting, or got worn down by hunger and thirst, the oblivion of endorphin helped him keep doing what it took to save himself.

"Runners high" is the well-known endorphin experience. But a regular daily run does not make you "high." You have to push beyond your capacity to the point of distressing your body to get that good feeling. This is not necessarily a good way to promote survival. Endorphin did not evolve to motivate you to inflict pain on yourself. It evolved to help you escape pain.

Perhaps you've seen a zebra wriggle out of the jaws of a lion on a wildlife documentary. You see the zebra run for its life with its flesh ripped open by the lion's teeth. Endorphin masks the pain for a few moments, which helps the zebra escape. If it fails to escape and ends up in the lion's jaw, it will die in an endorphin haze. Nature's euthanasia is nice to know about while you watch disturbing footage of predator devouring prey. Endorphin was not meant for partying but for momentary respite in the brutal struggle for life.

The respite is brief because pain has survival value. Pain is your body's signal that something is urgently wrong. If you ignored pain all the time, you would touch hot stoves and walk on broken legs. You would not make good survival choices if you were always high on endorphin. Masking pain promotes survival in narrow circumstances, but we evolved to notice distress signals, not to mask them with oblivion.

Endorphin is called the body's "natural morphine." The truth is the opposite: morphine is artificial endorphin. Opium derivatives, like heroin, make you high because they fit into the body's natural endorphin receptors.

Laughing triggers a bit of endorphin, and so does crying. The internal convulsions of laughing and crying cause physical distress. The distress is very brief so the burst of endorphin is too. This road to euphoria is limited. Fake laughs don't trigger the internal convulsions, and real laughs only last for seconds. Real cries are painful, and fake cries don't trigger the necessary bodily distress, despite the psychic distress.

Endorphin experiences	
List examples of a good feeling that masks physical pain, in yourself and others.	

© 2012 L. Breuning

Endorphin is different from adrenaline. Skydiving and bungee jumping trigger an "adrenaline high," because you anticipate pain. Adrenaline releases the energy you need to handle an emergency. The "adrenaline junkie" is not seeking pain– he seeks to avoid pain. The brain anticipates pain when it sees the ground rushing at you, so it releases a lot of adrenaline. When you're on a roller coaster in an amusement park, you tell yourself the threat isn't real. But your brain evolved in a world of real threats, not self-imposed, artificially concocted threats. When it sees lots of threat signals, it releases the adrenaline.

This book does not cover adrenaline because it does not cause happiness. It causes a state of arousal, as if your body is stepping on the gas. Some people get to like that feeling, but it is not a "good for you" signal from your mammal brain's perspective. It is simply a signal that something is extremely relevant to your survival, either good or bad. For example, if you are about to accept the Nobel Prize from the King of Sweden, a spurt of adrenaline tells you that the moment is important. The same spurt would alert you if your parachute didn't open. Adrenaline amplifies the positive or negative message conveyed by the other neurochemicals. It prepares you for immediate action, but it doesn't tell you whether that action should be going toward or running away.

Social pain does not trigger endorphin the way physical pain does, except for a brief laugh or cry. A broken heart doesn't trigger endorphin the way a broken bone does. In the past, daily life held so much physical pain that social pain was secondary. Today, we spend less time suffering the pain of physical labor, predator attack, or deteriorating disease. Our attention is free to focus on the pain of disappointed social expectations. This leaves us feeling that life is more painful even though it's less painful than in the past.

Meet Your Oxytocin

When you have a good feeling about someone, oxytocin causes it. When you feel you can trust a person, or you enjoy their trust in you, oxytocin is flowing. The feeling of belonging, and of safety in numbers, is oxytocin too.

Social trust improves survival prospects, and it feels good. The brain motivates you to build social bonds by rewarding them with a good feeling, and thus promotes survival.

Feeding a horse is a very simple example of the oxytocin feeling. When I walk toward a horse with food in my hand, I am not sure I want to put my fingers near those huge teeth. The horse is not sure he wants a stranger in his face. We check each other out slowly. Each brain is scanning for evidence that it's safe to trust. When both of us are satisfied that the other doesn't pose an immediate threat, we relax, and it feels good. That's the release of oxytocin.

Trust helps a horse survive in a crucial way. By trusting its herd-mates, a horse gets an extended alarm system. Each horse shares the burden of staying alert for predators. The horse that trusts his fellow horse is more likely to survive.

Mammals live in herds and packs and troops because there's safety in numbers. A mammal doesn't consciously decide whether to stick with the herd or strike out on his own when he wakes up each morning. Instead, his brain produces a good feeling near the group, and a bad feeling when separated. Cortisol surges when a herd animal can't see at least one of his group, and oxytocin surges when he's reunited with them.

Mammals leave the group when it promotes reproduction. Young mammals typically transfer to a new troop at puberty to improve mating opportunities.[1] A mother mammal risks leaving the group to search for a lost child and to give birth. Reproductive behaviors trigger even more oxytocin that mere companionship, which motivates a mammal to leave the group when it's good for his or her genes.

When a female gives birth, her oxytocin surges. This facilitates labor and lactation, and motivates her to guard the newborn constantly. Oxytocin also spikes in the newborn's brain, so a young mammal clings to its mother long before it comprehends the danger of leaving her. Attachment to the mother is the build-up of oxytocin circuits, and over time this attachment transfers to a herd or pack or troop.

Touch triggers oxytocin. Primates are often seen grooming each other, running their fingers through a troop-mate's fur to remove debris. The sensation feels good to both the giver and the receiver thanks to oxytocin. Primates invest lots of time grooming each other, and it appears to establish social alliances. When there's a conflict within a primate troop, monkeys and apes rush to the aid of the individuals they groom with. Researchers find that monkeys and apes with more social alliances get better mating opportunities and have more surviving offspring. The good feeling of oxytocin motivates social grooming and that promotes survival.

The down side of herd behavior is obvious to humans. We worry about jumping over cliffs when the other lemmings jump. We worry about group-think and gangs and co-dependence. Before you dismiss the herd impulse, it's important to understand its value in nature. A solitary mammal

---

1 Either the males or the females disperse at puberty, depending on the species.

is quickly eaten by a predator. It's hard to stay alert for predators all the time. Sticking with a herd distributes the burden of vigilance among many eyes and ears. To us, it seems foolish to run as soon as a herd-mate runs. But the mammal who refuses to run until he sees the lion for himself is less likely to survive. Brains that refused to trust got weeded out of the gene pool, and natural selection produced a brain that is able to trust its mates.

Reptiles, by contrast, stay alone in their vigilance. A reptile has no warm and fuzzy feelings toward other reptiles. Lizards don't trust other lizards. They have a chemical equivalent of oxytocin, but they only release it during mating and childbirth. Mammals release oxytocin (and variants that differ by an atom or two) more often, and we have lots of oxytocin receptors. Each release of oxytocin links all the neurons firing at the time. We associate the good feeling with those around us, and thus attachment builds.

Attachments make mammals what they are. We care for our young, which make it possible for our young to be born without survival skills. We learn from experience instead of being born pre-programmed. Reptiles, by contrast, strike out on their own the moment they're born. Instead of relying on parental care, a young lizard starts running the instant he hatches from his shell. If he doesn't run fast enough, a parent eats him— the better to recycle the energy into another sibling instead of letting a predator get it. Fish don't even wait for their eggs to hatch. They swim off the moment their eggs are fertilized, to pursue other interests. Plants send their seed into the wind and never find out whether it grows into mighty oaks.

Plants and fish and reptiles survive because they are born with hard-wired survival knowledge. Mammals are born fragile and stupid, but they learn from experience while under the protection of their elders. Instead of being born with a brain that develops in the safety of the uterus or egg, our brains develop by interacting with the world around us. This wires us to survive in the world we actually live in rather than the world of our ancestors.

The smaller an animal's brain, the more it survives on pre-wired knowledge. The bigger an animal's brain, the more it incorporates life experience into its survival strategy. A pre-wired brain is good at surviving in a specific ecological niche, and dies quickly outside that niche. A big brain is born ready to make connections rather than with the connections themselves.

The larger a creature's brain, the longer it remains fragile after birth, because it takes time to fill a brain with a network of connections. This creates a survival challenge because fragile newborns are easily eaten by predators. In older species, females gave birth to hundreds or thousands of offspring in order for a few to survive. But that makes it impossible to invest in each one. Mammals developed a very different strategy. We have very few children and do our darnedest to keep every single one alive.

This is a risky reproductive strategy. The more you invest in each child, the more you lose if it dies. Attachment is what makes this strategy possible. Mammalian mothers guard each newborn constantly, and herds help them protect the young from predators. When a mama mammal loses a child, she loses a big chunk of her lifetime reproductive capacity, but oxytocin keeps motivating attachment.

Not long ago, most humans spent their lives in the network of attachments they were born into. Now, many people disparage attachments. Without them, however, we feel like something is wrong. We don't know what it is, but we long for the place where "everybody knows your name." Or the concert and sports arena where thousands of people share your ups and downs from moment to moment. Or the political group that shares your anger. Or the online forum that welcomes your comments. These things feel good because social trust stimulates oxytocin. Of course, they are only brief moments of trust– small squirts of oxytocin that will soon pass. That's why the brain is always looking for a chance to get more of that oxytocin feeling.

Oxytocin experiences	
List examples of a good feeling triggered by social trust, in yourself and others.	

© 2012 L. Breuning

While trust feels good, betrayed trust feels awful. The bad feeling of disappointed trust motivates mammals to decide carefully when to trust and when to withhold trust. Big-brained primates are choosy about their friends. Instead of all-or-nothing attachment to a group, monkeys and apes have enough neurons to form individualized attachments with troop mates. They might make an oxytocin link with one social interaction and a cortisol link with the next. Over time, you "know who your friends are" because your neurochemicals react to individuals as "good for your survival" or "bad for your survival."

When you spend time with people, you can't help noticing that social alliances are constantly being negotiated. You may find it annoying when other people do it. But when you do it, you feel like you're just trying to survive. Social alliances transform a bad, threatened feeling into a good, safe feeling, thanks to oxytocin.

Monogamy is rare in the mammal world, except in animals known to have a high level of oxytocin (or its chemical equivalents). Monogamy is common among birds, who also engage in parental care and produce an oxytocin-equivalent. Most mammals form long-term bonds with foraging partners rather than sex partners. This promotes survival. You might have mixed feelings about the people you eat and work with. You might not trust them all the time and even wonder why you put up with them at all. But when you leave them, your oxytocin falls and your mammal brain tells you that something is wrong.

Meet Your Serotonin

Getting respect feels good because it triggers serotonin. The good feeling motivates you to seek more respect, and that promotes survival. You may say you don't care about getting respect, but you can easily see this dynamic in others. In the animal world, getting respect clearly promotes an individual's DNA. They're not thinking about genes, of course. Mammals seek social dominance because serotonin makes it feel good.

In one study, an alpha vervet monkey was placed behind a one-way mirror to deprive him of the respect he usually got from his troop-mates. The mirror was placed so that the alpha could see his troop-mates, but they couldn't see him. He made the dominance gestures typical of his species, but his subordinates did not respond with submission gestures. The alpha got agitated and his serotonin level fell. Each day the experiment continued, his serotonin kept dropping and his agitation grew. He needed their submission to keep up his serotonin.

All living creatures have serotonin, even amoeba. One-celled animals use it in a way that's curiously relevant to us. We humans have more serotonin in our digestive system than we have in our brains. An amoeba is too small for a separate digestive system and nervous system, but it uses serotonin in a way that helps us understand its dual purpose. Serotonin signals the amoeba's body to move toward food, and prepare to receive food. The mechanism is astonishingly simple. An amoeba constantly forages and scans for danger by letting tiny amounts of water pass through its cell membrane. If the water sample shows a high concentration of foreign material, the amoeba interprets that as danger and it wiggles away. If the sample contains a low level of foreign material, the amoeba perceives a feeding opportunity and releases serotonin. The neurochemical causes its digestive juices to flow and its tail to forge a course straight ahead. Serotonin is the amoeba's response to the perception that it's safe to feed.

In mammals, serotonin is the good feeling of having secure access to food or other resources. In a mammalian herd or pack or troop, food and mating opportunities are typically dominated by stronger individuals. This may seem to conflict with one's pristine view of nature. But close observation of countless species shows that each has its way of competing for resources. When animals cooperate it makes headlines, but much of the time animals are having food fights, battling over mating opportunities, and doing everything and anything to get their kids ahead. Humans strive to curb these impulses, but we've inherited a brain that rewards social dominance with serotonin.

Imagine a piglet born in a litter of sixteen to a mother who has twelve teats. Each piglet struggles for nourishment from the moment of birth. Complex decisions are required. The more a piglet struggles, the more energy it consumes. But without struggle, it starves to death. Serotonin mediates these decisions. Each time a piglet dominates another, it gets a squirt of serotonin. That feels good, which motivates it to dominate again. The more nourishment it gets, the more its dominance-seeking efforts are likely to succeed. If it fails to dominate, its serotonin falls. That also promotes survival by reducing its motivation to dominate, so it spends less energy and survives on the food it has. The ups and the downs of serotonin both promote survival, by balancing energy expenditure with food intake.

If the piglet got seriously malnourished, its cortisol would spike. That would promote survival by triggering aggression. Aggression is different from social dominance because cortisol feels bad while serotonin feels good. Social dominance is the calm, secure feeling that your needs will be met.

When a piglet has enough energy, it strives to dominate a teat. If it succeeds, it starts striving for a better teat– one that's closer to the mother's heart. What makes the top teats better than the hind teats is still being debated by researchers, but farmers have known for centuries that piglets struggle mightily to get a better one.

Mother Pig does not intervene in this conflict. The siblings sort it out for themselves in a few days. Each piglet learns from experience. It builds expectations about which behaviors are likely to bring pain and which are likely to get rewarded. When a piglet sees a safe chance to forge ahead and meet its needs, its serotonin flows.

Nice people don't talk about the competition for resources in nature. In polite society, it's forbidden to acknowledge that social dominance feels good. But everyone has a brain that longs for the good feeling of serotonin. Everyone can see this motivation in others. The point is not that you should push your way to the best teat. The point is that your brain constantly monitors your access to the resources you need to survive. When the access seems secure, you feel good. And then you look for ways to make things more secure.

You may get annoyed when you see others trying to secure their position. But when you do it, you think, "I'm just trying to survive."

Securing resources is complicated when you live in a group. A solitary reptile doesn't worry about what others will do when it finds a piece of food. It just lunges. But if group-living mammals all lunged at a bit of food, some of them would get hurt. The smaller, weaker ones would get hurt. Avoiding injury promotes survival more than any one bit of food. So each brain monitors those around it and decides whether it's stronger or weaker before it acts on the impulse to eat. When it's weaker, it restrains itself until the other has eaten. When a mammal sees that it's stronger, its serotonin surges and it lunges at the food. It has to eat when it can in order to survive. [2]

Studies "proving" that animals are altruistic often make the news. There's a big demand for evidence that nature is good, and researchers create a supply that meets the demand. In the name of science, hundreds of trials are done, and only the instances that can be construed as altruism are reported. Often, they emerge from artificial situations concocted in a laboratory. When adult animals snatch food from the mouths of juveniles in their daily routine, you don't hear about it in the news.

Young mammals quickly learn to avoid injury by submitting to stronger individuals. Being dominated hurts, and the cortisol it triggers wires a youth to avoid conflict. That may look like "cooperation" to the casual observer, but the animal still wants its chance to eat and reproduce. So it seizes opportunities where it's likely to win without getting injured. I am not saying we should dominate the weak. I am saying each brain is focused on meeting its needs.

Animals can't save money for a rainy day. The only way they can put something aside for the future is to invest today's extra energy into social power that can help them survive tomorrow. That's why each mammalian herd or pack or troop has its status hierarchy. The organization is not conscious, of

---

2 Males and females seek social dominance in ways that best promote their DNA. In most mammals, a female's reproductive success is best served by behaviors that enhance the survivability of her offspring, while a male's reproductive success is served by maximizing mating opportunities. Within these strategies, male and female brains are still monitoring when their survival needs are best served by dominating and when by submitting.

course. Each individual simply remembers whom they fear and whom they trust, and a hierarchy emerges organically. Cortisol motivates each individual to hunch down in self-defense in the face of a stronger group-mate. And serotonin motivates it to relax and swell its chest swell with pride (or air, depending on how you look at it) when it is strong enough to get respect and meet its needs.

A cow who pushes her way to the center of the herd is safer from predators than a cow near the outer edge. The pushy cow improves her chances of living to reproduce and keeping her young alive. Bulls typically avoid the herd until mating time, when they ferociously battle other males for admission. The most dominant bull pushes his way to the center of the herd, where he meets and inseminates the most dominant cows. In each species, social dominance promotes reproductive success in one way or another. I am not advocating such behavior, but recognizing the effort it takes for humans to restrain these urges.

In the animal world, higher-status males generally get more mating opportunity. Higher-status females tend to be more fertile and their young have higher survival rates. Social dominance brought reproductive success, so brains that seek social dominance were naturally selected for.

Humans learn to restrain the dominance urge because that promotes social trust (oxytocin). Your brain is always trying ways to get more serotonin without losing oxytocin or increasing cortisol. For example, if your comment in a meeting gets respect, that feels good. But if you try to dominate the meeting, unfortunate side effects may catch up with you. Each time you get respect, your brain makes links that help you figure out how to get more. Each time you lose respect, your brain makes links that help you avoid losing it in the future.

Life experience wires each brain to perceive respect in its own way. If you set your sights on being master of the universe, you may end up feeling disrespected much of the time. Your life may be fine in objective terms, but if you expect continual admiration from others, you may experience a lot of disappointment. Another person might learn to feel satisfied with the respect they are getting from their world, and thus enjoy the calm, secure feeling of serotonin.

Serotonin experiences	
Examples of social respect triggering good feelings, at work, at play, in self and others.	

© 2012 L. Breuning

Social dominance is different from socio-economic status. A person who is #3 on the world billionaire list might feel like his survival is threatened when he falls to #4. By contrast, a person with little socio-economic status could harshly dominate those around him and feel good about it. Many social dominance strategies are unrelated to formal wealth and status. Appearance is a good example. One person may feel respected for their appearance, while another feels disrespected, even if the two people look the same. Our neurochemicals depend on the expectation circuits we've built.

Anti-depressants, like *Prozac*, are known for raising serotonin levels in the brain. The function of serotonin was not understood when anti-depressants were introduced to the public, in the same way that aspirin was used long before anyone knew how it worked. Now, animal studies offer insight into our neurochemical ups and downs. But these insights are unsettling. The dominance-seeking urges of mammals are not a simple antidote to depression. They are only a window into the value of circuits that trigger self-respect.

Each of the happy chemicals turns on for a specific, survival-relevant reason. Then it turns off so it's ready to react to the next survival opportunity that comes your way. When a happy-chemical spurt ends, unhappy chemicals get your attention. We strive to eliminate unhappy chemicals or at least mask them with happy chemicals. But unhappy chemicals are here to stay. The following chapter explains why.

2
Good Reasons to Be Unhappy

Unhappy Chemicals Are Nature's Security Alarm

When you see a lizard basking in the sun, it looks like the picture of happiness. But that lizard is just trying to avoid death. Cold-blooded reptiles must sun themselves often or they die of hypothermia. But when a lizard goes out in the sun, he risks being eaten alive by a predator. So he shuttles constantly between the lethal threats of sun and shade.

And his brain is perfectly adapted for the job. It releases cortisol when his temperature is dangerously low, which motivates him to go out sunning. But as soon as his body reaches a safe temperature, he runs back to the good feeling of a safe hiding spot. While he's exposed and vulnerable, his brain constantly scans for predators, ready to run at the slightest whiff. He is not having fun yet. But he survives, because his brain is skilled at weighing one threat against another.

You have the brain of a reptile at the base of your limbic system. Mammals built on top of reptilian brain structures rather than starting from scratch. The systems we added release happy chemicals to mediate social life. But we still use the reptile brain for the jobs it is good at, like alerting the body to potential harm. Nature adapts old parts rather than starting over.

Your brain stem and cerebellum are eerily similar to a reptile's brain.[1] You are good at avoiding survival threats because your brain releases cortisol when something looks bad. Of course, you can make fine judgments about potential threats because your cortex brings its huge information-processing capacity to the job. But your cortex cannot make judgments without your neurochemicals. It sees the world as a mass of detail until neurochemicals mark things as good for you or bad for you. Your cortex is always working together with your older brain systems. You need your reptile brain to avoid harm.

Cortisol is the brain's emergency broadcast system. Corticoid hormones are produced by reptiles, amphibians, fish and even worms, when they encounter survival threats. It makes them feel bad, and motivates them to "do something, now."

Cortisol is what humans call "pain." Pain gets your attention. It feels bad because that succeeds at getting your attention. Once you experience pain, you don't want to experience it again. Your brain strives to avoid pain by storing details of the experience, so you know what to look out for in the future. When you see things associated with past pain, your cortisol is triggered and you get ready to do what it takes to avoid more pain.

A big burst of cortisol is what we call "fear." Small drips of cortisol are "anxiety" or "stress." These bad feelings tell you you're in immediate danger of pain, and your cortex tries to figure out what the danger is. Your reptile brain can't say why it

---

1 Reptiles also have a limbic system and cortex, but they're tiny.

released the cortisol. It just responds when electricity flows down a pathway you connected in the past. You built those pathways from real experience, so the danger feels real to you. You want to avoid stress, but you want to avoid harm even more.

Bad feelings are often caused by real threats, so avoiding bad feelings promotes survival. Cortisol does its job by motivating us to do what it takes to eliminate bad feelings. We dream of a life with no bad feelings, and a world in which everything that makes us feel bad is gone. But our brains will keep releasing cortisol. We need it to avoid real risks as much as we need happy chemicals to steer us toward rewards. Sometimes we may over-react to threats, and other times we may mask threats with happy chemicals. Survival threats are not perfectly predictable, so we need both our neurochemical warning system and our information-processing cortex.

Valuing Unhappiness

When a cautious reptile brain is hooked up to a dominance-seeking mammal brain and a pattern-seeking human cortex, it's not surprising that alarm signals are triggered a lot. If you expect to eliminate unhappy chemicals from your life, you are likely to be disappointed. You are better off accepting the part that unhappy chemicals play in human life. Cortisol is not just the cause of unnecessary pain. Much of the time, it succeeds at preventing pain.

For example, lizards run from me the moment I walk out my door. Most of the time they are running for nothing because I would never step on a lizard. But who knows how many lizards have saved their lives from my accidental footsteps.

Reptiles protect themselves from the faintest danger signal without faulting themselves for it. False positives are part of the reptilian survival system.

Humans hate false positives. We expect to duck every bullet, but we hate to duck when there is no bullet. We expect our alarm system to call the shots perfectly every time. I think about this when I watch the meerkats at the zoo. They run for cover whenever a plane flies overhead. Their fear seems misguided since the plane is not an eagle who could eat them. But meerkats did not evolve to live in zoos near airports. They evolved in places where birds of prey could grab them in an instant. They survived because of their alertness for a particular pattern of cues. I am not saying we should fear everything our ancestors feared. I am simply appreciating the meerkats' self-acceptance. They don't castigate themselves for their timidity after the plane passes. They don't berate each other for bad calls. They just go back to what they were doing before the plane passed: scanning for threats and opportunities.[2]

We humans also use excess caution to avoid harm. For example, I wash my hands before every meal even though no deadly bacteria are there most of the time. I look in my rearview mirror whenever I change lanes even though no car is there much of the time. You might wear seat-belts your whole life without ever being in an accident. Anticipating potential threats helps us prevent unhappiness in the long run.

But if I wanted to protect myself from every possible danger signal, I could end up with endless hand-washing, mirror-checking habits. Sometimes it's better to approach

---

2 This is not to say that meerkats are always happy. They have plenty of conflict and violence, both within groups and between groups.

threats and gather information about them instead of avoiding them automatically. Cortisol helps you do that. It alerts you to new risks, which frees you to try new things and still notice when you've gone too far.

Accepting bad feelings sounds harsh, but the alternative is worse. You end up unhappy about being unhappy if you don't accept your own warning system. It's a vicious cycle of unhappy chemicals. The alternative is to accept your brain's reaction to anything similar to past threats. Some of those threats will be real and some won't, and you can't always predict correctly.

My security alarm	
Unhappiness I avoid with habits	
Unhappiness I accept as it comes	

© 2012 L. Breuning

When I wish my cortisol would stop, I think about feral pigs. These are pigs who have escaped from farms and returned to the wild. They start developing the features of wild boars once they start meeting their own survival needs. Their snouts grow long when they use those snouts to root for food. Their fur grows long when they need it for shelter from the cold. I am not saying we should act like wild boars. I am saying our efforts to meet our needs make us who we are. A farm pig has the potential to be a boar, but doesn't express the traits when its needs are met by a farmer. A domesticated pig has traits of a juvenile wild boar because it hasn't faced the survival challenges that develop mature traits. Survival challenges are not evidence that something has gone wrong with the world. They're evidence that you are a free adult rather than a farm animal.

Do Something, Or Else

Cortisol does its job by making you feel like you will die if you don't act instantly. Of course, you know you won't actually die if you fail to get that hoped-for promotion, or if someone pulls your hair on the playground. You know you won't die if there's a long line at the post office and you end up getting a parking ticket. But your neurochemicals evolved for life-or-death challenges, so when they start flowing, you feel like catastrophe is around the corner if you don't "do something" immediately.

Sometimes you can't see a way to "do something." Modern life is not the cause of this problem. Our ancestors faced threats with no instant fix, too. When they escaped lions at the water hole, they had to face the water hole the next day. If you had lived in the past, sores would have irritated your skin, and vermin would have infested your home, your food, and your drinking water. You would have watched siblings die, and neighbors invade, rape and pillage. You would not have been free to choose your own sex partners. You would have lived with a lot of unhappy chemicals. And you would have kept looking for ways to "do something" to feel better.

Why do so many people believe their lives are harder than life in other times and places? Because neurochemicals get your attention more than facts. If you are worried about taking the SATs or looking fat, cortisol tells you that something is urgently wrong. You might have faced bigger threats elsewhere, but such threats feel less real to your brain. Other lives may seem like paradise because they don't have SATs or diets– the threats you wired yourself to respond to. You may think animals are happy because they don't have your problems, even though they go hungry for days and have food and mates grabbed from them by stronger individuals. Consciously, you know that looking fat is not as bad as famine and plague. You know that an irritable boss is not as bad as invasion and rape by a neighboring tribe. But if you never actually felt the threat of plague or invasion, it doesn't sound as bad as your moody boss or your weight gain.

We don't realize the extent to which our perceptions of danger are wired from past experience. These circuits are quirky because experience is never a random sample of the world at large. A great example is the story of a girl who panicked when she heard laughter. The girl had been in a car accident and awoke from a coma to learn that some of her friends had died. She did not remember the accident, but she began having panic attacks at the sound of laughter. A therapist helped her remember that she was laughing and partying in the back of the car at the moment of impact. Her reptile brain connected the pain of the accident to the sound that went with it. Of course the girl knows in her cortex that laughter doesn't cause car crashes. But large amounts of pain create large cortisol circuits without the cortex getting involved. Now, when her brain hears laughter, it sounds the alarm in attempt to avoid a painful car crash. The alarm tells her she must do something urgently, but the message doesn't make sense so she doesn't know what to do.

The reptile brain's quirky way of interpreting danger makes sense when you look at it from a lizard's perspective. Imagine a lizard being seized by an eagle. Claws dig into his sides, triggering cortisol and fusing all the neurons active at that moment. If the lizard manages to free himself and survive, he will have neural pathways that efficiently release cortisol when they perceive the sights, sounds and smells that were active when the pain was experienced. That includes everything the reptile experienced a moment *before* the pain, because those neurons are still electrically active. The lizard links danger to the smell of the eagle as it swooped in, and the sudden darkness caused by the eagle blocking out the sun. In the future, the lizard will run faster when he detects that smell and that shadow. And he will survive.

From a survival perspective, the inputs you experience just before a moment of pain are the essential information. They enable you to recognize advance warning signals and thus avoid harm. The brain stores such information without conscious effort or intent because sensory inputs remain electrically active for a moment before they extinguish. This "buffer memory" allows pain circuits to include the events that preceded the pain. It allows creatures to detect probable threats without need for rational analysis. Cortisol builds circuits that motivate a reptile to avoid death without actually "knowing" what death is or what an eagle is. Our brains do the same. We get wired for advance warning signs of the dangers we actually experienced. When big cortisol spurts cause big warning circuits, we label it "post-traumatic stress." But smaller cortisol spurts are always building smaller warning circuits that we're less aware of.

Sometimes our warning circuits don't make useful predictions. It would be nice if we could delete them, but there's a good survival reason why we can't. Imagine your ancestor watching someone die from eating a poison berry. His cortisol would surge and he would remember what that berry looked like forever. If he was hungry decades later and could find nothing to eat but that berry, the enduring cortisol circuit would help him resist. Your ancestor survived because he honored his neurochemical impulses.

Today, we like to challenge old fears. You might like to imagine your ancestor courageously eating that berry and proving that it was harmless all along. But in practice, someone who ignored warning signals as soon as he got hungry would have died and his genes would have disappeared. Our genes come from people who held onto their experiential learning. Once you experience a pain yourself, your brain does not let go of that information.

This mechanism may seem flawed, but learning from experience is much more efficient than being hard-wired for dangers at birth. Instead of being born to fear things that threatened our ancestors, each generation of humans is able to learn about danger from its own cortisol experiences. To some extent, we learn about danger from our elders. But each generation builds its own fears and tends to sneer at the fears of its elders.

I learned this in a painful way. My mother once told me she couldn't sleep all night because she worried that she forgot to put the milk back in the refrigerator and feared it would spoil on the counter overnight. I sneered at her anxiety. But after she died, I realized that when she was a child, she would have gone hungry if she left the milk out. Her three sisters would have gone hungry too, because she was responsible for feeding them when she was only a child herself. Real pain built connections in her brain that were always there.

Danger circuits I've built	
The ones that serve me well	
The ones I would love to delete	

© 2012 L. Breuning

I wish I had understood this when she was alive. The best I can do is celebrate my brain's ability to learn from my own experience. I didn't have to learn everything from scratch. My cortisol was triggered when I saw the fear of others, thanks to my mirror neurons. That saved me from having to learn by playing in traffic and eating poison berries. But each baby born into the world gets to build her own threat detector.

The human brain generalizes from past dangers. Sometimes we over-react, but we'd be worse off if we didn't generalize. If a jellyfish touched a hot stove, only the tentacle that got burned would learn from the experience. Jellyfish don't have a central nervous system, so one hand literally doesn't know what the other hand is doing. Your brain is a big central clearing house that generalizes from past pain to potential future pain. We anticipate threats so efficiently that we start worrying today about statistical projections of harm to one person per ten million twenty years from now. We feel anxiety when the boss lifts one eyebrow by one millimeter. It's frustrating to be so good at anticipating harm.

Mammals developed a way to alleviate the unpleasant feeling of imminent threat. They congregate in groups. Herds make it easier to relax while remaining alert for danger. Herd behavior has a bad ring to it, but the math proves that safety in numbers promotes survival better than the every-reptile-for-himself lifestyle. Mammals have a higher life expectancy than most earlier species, and their babies have a much higher survival rate. This has tremendous consequences. Mammal mamas can have fewer offspring and invest more in each one. Maternal investment allows mammals to have brains that learn from experience instead of being born pre-programmed.

But life is not all warm and fuzzy in the mammal world. Social groups trigger bad feelings as well as good feelings. When the brain adapted to group life, a new kind of unhappiness evolved: social pain.

Social Pain and the Mammal Brain

Social pain is like physical pain because it warns you of a survival threat. In the state of nature, you need social bonds to survive, and the brain evolved to give you an emergency alert when it sees a threat to your social bonds.

Social pain is not new to the modern world. Your ancestors suffered when group-mates rejected them, or dominated them callously. Chimpanzees do too. If your life is full of real pain from hunger, violence, hard labor, and disease, social pain doesn't command your attention. But when your brain finds no immediate physical threat, it focuses on social threats. Every possible threat to your social bonds and status looms large in your mind.

The social pain you experienced in the past triggered cortisol, which connected neurons. Now your brain is skilled at seeing the advance warning signs of that particular social threat. A cortisol alert is easily released at the slightest hint of that old familiar pain.

Animals sometimes eject an individual from the group. The most common examples are deposed alphas and adolescent males. Cortisol spikes in the ostracized animal, and indeed they often perish. Animals fear exclusion so intensely that they typically do what it takes to stay with the group, even when dominated harshly.

Everyone has past experience with social pain. We are all born dependent on others for our survival. As children, we learn to seek support from others when we're threatened. But sooner or later, that support wanes. A species would die out if the young did not learn to survive before their parents die. When a mammal loses the protection of his elders, the perceived risk triggers cortisol. That wires him to react to losing social support in the future.

You may not consciously believe you will die without support. But your limbic system releases feelings that surprise you. For example, if your work is criticized at a performance review, you know your survival is not literally threatened, but your cortisol rises. This wires you to scan for that particular threat, so you may see lots of evidence that fits.

Reptiles never worry about social exclusion. Mammals worry about it all the time. Herd animals constantly monitor the location of their group mates. Their cortisol rises when they cannot see others, and their oxytocin flows when they're surrounded by the group. The good feeling motivates them to seek safety in numbers without conscious intent. Mammals that were indifferent to the group were soon eaten by predators and got weeded out of the gene pool. The brain we've inherited was naturally selected to monitor social bonds all the time, and to feel bad at hints of threat to those bonds. Of course, you value your individuality. You don't just stick with the herd. But huge cortisol spikes seem to come from nowhere when you see threats to your social bonds.

The mammal brain is always monitoring what others are doing because that promotes survival. When leaving the group promotes survival even more, that's what a mammal does. Finding a lost child or improving mating prospects are the most common examples. Cortisol surges when you leave the group because the risk is real. But when your legacy is at stake, your brain motivates you to persevere despite the cortisol. You expect a big happy-chemical reward.

Social pain happens when you're inside a group as well as when you're outside, as we all know. Imagine you are a wildebeest in the vanguard of a herd looking for greener pastures. You reach a river and you stop, knowing that a crocodile will cause you pain if you jump in first. The rest of the herd stops behind you. Soon, a huge crowd builds up and you fear they will push you in. That would be more dangerous than jumping in, so you decide to take the plunge. As soon as you do, all those beyond you jump too. Crocodiles eat stragglers, so every wildebeest is determined not to be the one left behind. What looks like herd behavior results from individual survival calculations from moment to moment. Your survival is constantly affected by the choices of those around you.

Your brain is constantly choosing between preserving social bonds and striking out on your own. Cortisol helps you decide which option best promotes your survival. You may get a bad feeling when you think of the opportunities you lose by sticking with the herd. But you also get a bad feeling when you think of being isolated. Bad feelings are the brain's way of weighing one risk against others. We need bad feelings to interpret information, even when things are good. For example, you might be offered a great promotion in another state. You feel bad at the thought of losing the life you have now, but you feel bad about losing the career advancement. Unhappy chemicals help your brain calculate your best option.

Animals with bigger brains have more social ups and downs. Small-brained mammals tend to size up each other once, and stick with that circuit for life. Primates have enough neurons to keep updating their feelings about each other.

Primates are born with special neurons that facilitate social bonds. These *mirror neurons* activate when an individual watches the behavior of others. Scientists discovered mirror neurons by accident. They were studying the electrical activity in a monkey's brain while it grasped a peanut. When the experiment was over, a researcher picked up the peanut to put it away. To his amazement, the monkey's brain lit up with the same pattern of electricity it had when he picked up the peanut himself. Watching stimulates the same neural trails as acting.

Mirror neurons are not activated by watching random movement in others. They fire when you see others seek rewards or risk pain. Watching triggers much less electricity than doing. About 15% of the neurons are estimated to be mirror neurons in certain parts of the primate brain. But if you repeatedly watch another person, connections build and it becomes easier for you to execute the behavior yourself. This research is in its infancy, but there are indications that song birds learn their songs through mirror neurons.

Empathy comes from mirror neurons. We can literally feel other people's pain. If you repeatedly watch another person suffer, you build up your own circuit for experiencing that suffering. Even if you have a perfectly good life, those circuits make it easy for your cortisol to start flowing. The cortisol gives you the feeling that your survival is threatened, so your cortex looks for information about the threat. It will find threats, because that eases the nagging "do something" feeling. Social groups build a shared sense of threat as a result.

You can choose whether to focus your attention on these shared threat signals or not. But there's so safe choice. If you fail to empathize with shared pain, your social bonds are likely to be threatened. Your group-mates may start perceiving *you* as the threat. It's not easy being a primate.

Each brain builds expectations from the information it is fed. If you feed your brain a lot of inputs about suffering, you will build circuits good at finding more suffering. The world will look very bad to you. Your good intentions will leave you with a lot of cortisol.

Being Heard Equals Survival to the Human Brain

Exclusion makes a mammal unhappy, but inclusion does not necessarily make you happy. Once you're included, your brain wants more. It wants the attention of the group. You may be respectful of others, but part of your brain feels you will die if you do not get attention. We start out in life needing attention to survive, and cortisol wires us to fear losing it.

When you were born, your survival needs caused you pain, but you couldn't do anything about it. The resulting surge of cortisol caused you to cry, and that worked. It got your needs met. A newborn doesn't cry as a conscious act of communication. It doesn't cry because it knows what milk is. Crying is one of our few pre-wired behaviors. Soon, a baby learns to expect relief when he hears footsteps, and the expectation of attention stops the crying.

But a baby learns that attention can vanish as quickly as it came. The more a baby learns to expect support, the more he ventures out to explore the world, and thus the more threats he encounters. No amount of nurturing can protect a person from the reality of human vulnerability.

Your early vulnerability built the first circuits in your brain. Those old circuits are triggered today when your poetry is ignored by the one you love, or your views are ignored at a meeting. We don't consciously think being seen and heard is a matter of life or death. But our inevitable cortisol circuits make it feel that way.

The fragility of a newborn human is unparalleled in nature. No other creature is born so far from being able to survive on his own. A gazelle can run with the herd the day after he's born. An elephant can walk before his first meal, because that's how he gets to the nipple. A fish is an orphan from birth because his parents swim off once their eggs are fertilized. But the fish is born with fully developed survival circuits A human cannot even lift his head for weeks, and he can't provide for himself and his offspring for...decades.

We humans are born with an unfinished nervous system. Instead of developing fully *in utero,* we get born premature while our brain can still fit through the birth canal. Human brains grew bigger as our ancestors succeeded at getting more protein and fat.[3] Bigger brains led to better hunting methods, more nutrition, and even bigger brains. So our species got born at ever earlier stages of development, with lots of neurons, but fewer connections between them.

A chimpanzee is more hooked up at birth than a human, so its eyes and limbs start working quickly. A chimpanzee born prematurely looks amazingly similar to a newborn human. A full-term chimp is born with a brain already linked to his sensory organs and musculoskeletal system. Humans build these links outside the womb from direct experience. When a newborn human sees a hand flying in front of his face, he does not know he's attached to that hand, no less that he can control it. We are born helpless and we hook up our brains gradually during a long period of dependency. This gives us the advantage of adapting our nervous system to the environment we're born into, whereas animals are born adapted to one ecosystem and rarely survive outside it.

The vulnerability of a human baby is a huge survival challenge. Many babies died in the past. If they were good at

---

3 Even before they excelled at hunting, they learned to get marrow by scavenging bones.

getting attention, they were more likely to survive. Mothers good at interpreting their babies' signals had more surviving DNA. As a result, humans were naturally selected for the ability to communicate. When we succeed, happy chemicals flow. When we fail, cortisol flows and we look for a way to do something about it. Eventually, we develop complex communication circuits, but they rest on the core sense that you will die if you are not heard. You don't think this in words but you think it with neurochemicals.

The bad feeling of being ignored is compounded when you see others getting attention. In every troop of primates, some individuals get more attention than others. Field researchers have documented the way baboons give their attention to some troop-mates more than others. Laboratory researchers find that chimpanzees will exchange food for a chance to look at photos of the alpha chimp in their group. Your brain seeks attention as if your life depended on it because in the state of nature, it does. Cortisol flows when the expectation is disappointed.

The Unquenchable Thirst for Status

Respect makes people happy, and disrespect makes people unhappy. We tell ourselves status doesn't matter and everyone is equal, but each brain keeps track of how it stacks up against others. Expectations build from experience, making people sensitive to slights. Happy chemicals flow when our expectations are exceeded. When our expectations are disappointed, we perceive it as a threat.

Everyone wants to be special. When you see others being special, you say you want equality. When someone gets ahead of you, your cortisol starts flowing. It's easy to see this in others, especially those you dislike. It's hard to see it in yourself, but the universality of this urge is apparent when you know how animals strive to be special.

Animals one-up each other in myriad ways, and each way somehow promotes reproductive success. A simple example is the way animals make themselves look bigger by making their hair stand on end. They don't do it consciously, but when their cortisol is triggered they get goose bumps, which causes their hair follicles to tighten. That makes their hair stand out, giving adversaries the impression they are bigger than they are. Looking big promotes survival, and bad feelings make it happen.

The bigger a mammal's brain, the more effort it invests in the quest for social status. Small-brained animals like cows generally have one status ranking for life. When a cow reaches puberty or joins a new herd, she fights each other cow once.[4] If she wins, she learns that she can dominate that individual, and if she loses, she learns to submit to that individual to avoid injury. Her brain links each herd-mate to either her cortisol or her serotonin. A herd is typically dominated by an "alpha," who is the unchallenged queen for life. When she dies, the high-status cows will challenge each other for her spot. Then things go back to normal. Cows don't have enough neural plasticity to keep updating their circuits.

Primates do. Monkeys and apes tend to challenge their place in the status hierarchy. That doesn't mean they fight all the

---

4 Female bovine live in herds. Males tend not to in their natural state as opposed to the hormonally-altered domesticated state.

time. They avoid fighting because they can anticipate pain. Instead, they build social alliances that threaten their adversaries with pain. Primates find ways to get along because their unhappy chemicals warn them that conflict is dangerous. But the primate brain is always on the lookout for safe ways to raise its rank.

If a monkey or ape shows weakness, others are quick to notice the opportunity and challenge them. Successful challenges stimulate serotonin and create more surviving offspring with better survival prospects. Brains that seek status were thus selected for.

Animals care about the status of their mating partners. Each species has its own strategies for judging potential mates, and biologists have shown that the traits animals focus on are uncannily relevant to the survival potential of offspring. For example, peacocks with more colorful tails actually have higher resistance to deadly parasites, which gives their children a survival advantage.

Research has made it clear that each primate in a group is aware of the relative status of each troop-mate in relation to others as well as to themselves. And after an internal conflict, each primate brain rewires itself to reflect the new status hierarchy. The rewards for status are often quite small, but they get the brain's attention when it's not busy meeting a more urgent survival need. Brains good at status-seeking made more copies of themselves, and the rest is history.

You may say you don't care about status. But your happy chemicals soar when you have the chance to mate with a high-status person, or the chance to raise your children's status, or any other status-booster that comes your way. Your unhappy chemicals soar when your specialness is overlooked, or, much worse, your children's specialness is overlooked. You may blame your disappointments on "our society" without recognizing its universality. If everyone in the room has eyes for the same beauty, many people will be unhappy. If everyone wants their children to go to the same few schools, lots of cortisol will flow. If everyone wants to be chief, unhappiness will reign. That does not mean everyone's survival is threatened, but each brain feels as if it is.

The urge to be special	
Disappointment of that urge in myself.	
Disappointment of that urge in others.	

© 2012 L. Breuning

Your feelings about your status are independent of your socio-economic circumstances. Imagine you're a high-priced lawyer with lots of formal status trappings. Every minute of your waking life you are kowtowing to clients and senior partners and people who can help your career. Wherever you look, you see threats that could cost you everything. You might feel worse about your status than a bus driver who rules the bus all day and then rules the roost at home. Status does not come from fixed labels and abstract words. It's the feeling you get when you interact with others. Those feelings change from moment to moment as we go through our day, but they depend heavily on the circuits you've already built.

Your brain compares itself to others even if you wish it didn't. In the state of nature, comparing yourself to others promotes survival. It protects you from getting into fights you are likely to lose. When your brain sees you are weaker than another individual, it releases cortisol to remind you of the risk. This helps you hold back, despite your urge to promote your survival interests. Unhappy chemicals help us inhibit our urge for dominance and thus get along with group mates. We need unhappy chemicals, as much as we'd rather live without them.

The Unhappiness of the Cortex

The intelligence of the human cortex adds to the unhappiness of the mammal brain. A meerkat may over-react to passing airplanes, but it never imagines planes that aren't there. Humans imagine potential future risks because it helps us prevent them. The things we imagine feel as real as the external inputs triggering our senses. We humans can scare ourselves with our own neurons!

Our ability to process abstractions leads us to understand our own mortality. We don't know what will kill us but we know we will die. This is plenty of incentive to keep scanning for threats.

Our skill at predicting harm helps us prevent it. But as soon as we eliminate one threat, our brain looks for another. So even if you're a very effective survivor, your cortisol flows.

Finding threats makes you feel curiously safe. When you know a lion is near, you feel safer when you can see it. We keep seeking evidence of threats, and we get a dopamine boost when we find what we seek. You may also get a serotonin boost from the feeling of being right, and an oxytocin boost if the evidence bonds you to those with similar concerns. This is why people seem oddly pleased to find evidence of doom and gloom.

A steady stream of cortisol leaves you feeling you must "do something" immediately to avoid disaster. But nothing you do stops the cortisol because you are generating it with your own thoughts.

Thinking about the future triggers the most threatening thought of all: the fact that the world will some day go on without you. This is so upsetting that people almost prefer imaging that the world will end when they end. I noticed this at a lecture on future energy reserves. When the audience was shown a chart projecting world energy reserves a hundred years from now, everyone had to imagine a world they would not be part of. This triggers cortisol, and we look for a logical explanation. We presume the crisis is in the world because we don't know what is triggering us. A big cortex attached to a reptile brain easily concludes that the world is going to hell in a handbasket.

A human cortex is good at predicting rewards as well as pain. When anticipated rewards don't materialize, more pain is triggered. Your cortex can imagine a better world that makes you happy all the time. But reality falls short of the better world of your imagination, so reality is a continual disappointment. We create this disappointment because we have enough neurons to build a world in our heads that feels as real as the world reaching our senses. In our imagined world, social and physical pain are easily eliminated, so it's hard to understand why the world you experience fails to measure up.

A lizard never thinks something is wrong with the world. It watches its young get eaten alive without telling itself "something must be done about this." It doesn't have enough neurons to imagine the world being anything other than what it is. It doesn't expect a world in which there are no predators, so it doesn't condemn the world for falling short of its expectations. Nor does it condemn itself for failing to keep every one of its offspring alive.

The world of the cortex	
Unhappiness created by anticipating harm	
Unhappiness created by anticipating rewards	

© 2012 L. Breuning

A monkey isn't thinking something is wrong with the world when he cedes a banana to the alpha monkey. He feels bad because his unhappy chemicals are triggered, and he tries to feel good by staying alert for opportunities to get bananas. But he isn't lamenting the state of the world.

Your brain's ability to imagine good things is unlimited. As soon as you get something good, your brain imagines more good things. Your potential to be disappointed is unlimited as a result. Reality can't live up to your expectations because you keep building new expectations. So even as your expectations lead you to better things, your cortisol flows and your survival feels threatened. That bad feeling keeps motivating you to focus on the "better world" you've constructed in your mind.

Your brain would be happy if you could control everything and live forever. That doesn't happen, so unhappy chemicals are part of life.

3

From Vicious Circle To Virtuous

The Quest To Stimulate Happy Chemicals

Imagine you're receiving an honorary doctorate from the Institute of Human Accomplishment. A huge audience applauds wildly as you express your gratitude. You feel great. A few minutes later, however, the ceremony is over and your happy chemicals are reabsorbed. You trigger some more when you reminisce, but you are soon back to who you were before the ceremony.

When a happy chemical surge is over, you notice your unhappy chemicals again. That prompts you to scan for threats. Was my speech well-received? Why did my friends miss it? Who will like my next accomplishment?

The world is full of potential threats, but you notice them less while happy chemicals are spurting. Once the spurt fades, unhappy chemicals grab your attention. You wonder how to get the good feeling back. Getting another honorary doctorate seems the way to go because you've built a huge connection.

Your brain is always looking for ways to feel good. Often, that leads to things that are good for you. Sleep feels good when you're tired, and warmth feels good when you're cold. Life is simple when you can relieve unhappy chemicals by doing things that feel good.

When that doesn't work, any way of feeling good seems enticing. Things that worked in the past come to mind. Maybe your bottle cap collection, or your Great Aunt Hilda. The brain expects things that felt good before to feel good again.

Your bottle cap collection can't protect you from harm, of course. But when your brain is screaming "do something," anything that triggers happy chemicals masks unhappy chemicals. Distraction is not the best survival strategy when your cortisol is triggered by a lion. But when your boss is in a bad mood, it's nice to have a way to mask your bad feelings.

Our happy chemical strategies are often a mystery to us. Why does your bottle cap collection give you pleasure while a fishing trip does nothing for you? Each brain learns from the experiences it has. If a child pulls out his collection on a day when he's experiencing a lot of pain, and then the pain stops, his brain "learns" that focusing on the collection stops pain. Each of us learns ways of stopping pain and turning on happy chemicals. We don't learn by intellectually analyzing every possible action. We learn from accidents of experience.

Often, the strategies we pick up are useful. When I was a child, I read books because it distracted me from what was going on around me. I did not think of reading as a way to promote my long-term survival. No one encouraged me to read. Indeed, it was considered rebellious and lazy. When I saw the hostility it provoked in my mother, I was more motivated to distract myself with books. Fortunately for me, that strategy had survival value.

But every strategy disappoints you because it never makes you as happy as it did at first.

And every happy strategy has side effects, which add up when you repeat it.[1]

We're motivated to repeat a strategy anyway because we want more happy chemicals.

Side effects may accumulate to the point where they stimulate unhappy chemicals. A vicious cycle results, as you keep seeking happy chemicals with a behavior that causes more unhappiness.

Happy chemicals disappoint for a good reason. They evolved to excite you about new rewards, not to waste your attention on the same old reward. Discovering a new planet would excite you, but looking at your planet every day would not re-kindle the initial excitement. If you expected to live at that level of excitement forever, you would be disappointed.

I feel a thrill when I walk into a coffee-roasting shop. Sometimes I comment on the delicious smell to the person behind the counter, and I realize they don't notice it. They have habituated to the fabulous smell. If I went to work at a coffee roaster in order to feel constant joy, I would be disappointed.

But such disappointment is hard to avoid, because your brain builds expectations when something feels good. This chapter describes the disappointment each happy chemical leads to. We'll explore dopamine disappointment, oxytocin disappointment, endorphin disappointment and serotonin disappointment.

Your brain doesn't give up after a disappointment. It tries again. It trusts its own circuits because they come from its own experience. If you had a great time at a party after you got a

---

1 More on this in my forthcoming book, **Confessions of a Travel Addict**.

bad grade in math, your brain built a link that suggests partying when you feel bad about math. The same parties will not make you as happy as they once did, however, and bad grades may pile up and make you more unhappy. You might respond by partying even more. You could build a new circuit that helps you feel good about doing your math homework. If you don't, the vicious circle is likely to continue.

Vicious cycles I have known	:|
Happy habits that mask unhappy chemicals	
Side effects that trigger more unhappiness	

© 2012 L. Breuning

You can probably think of ten vicious cycles in ten seconds: junk food, alcohol, love affairs, drugs, losing your temper, gaming, getting recognition, shopping, watching a screen, telling other people what to do, withdrawing, career advancement, pleasing people, climbing mountains, rescuing people, smoking, writing another book. (That's more than ten. I couldn't stop.)[2] All of these things can make you feel good, which motivates you to activate them over and over. But the

---

2 I don't use the word "addiction" here because it already has many connotations. Our goal is to understand neurochemical ups and downs in a new way.

good feeling doesn't mask unhappy chemicals as much as you expect, and the side effects feel bad. When you look for a way to feel better, the same happy strategy comes to mind. It has disappointed you before, but the highway to your happy chemicals is still there.

Happy chemicals were not meant to create constant ecstasy. They were meant to steer us toward things that promote survival. When we try to get constant happiness from them, disappointment is likely.

Dopamine Disappointment

The first lick of an ice cream cone is heaven. Ten licks later, your attention wanders. You start thinking about the next thing on your agenda, and the next. You still love the ice cream, but you don't feel it as much because it's not new information. Your brain is looking for the next great way to meet your needs. Dopamine is triggered by new rewards. Old rewards, even incredibly creamy-delicious ones, don't command your brain's attention. Scientists call this *habituation*.

How can a person be happy all the time with a brain designed to habituate to good things? Philosophers and poets have long contemplated this dilemma, and now scientists and even gastronomists are getting into the act. The top-rated restaurant in America is based on the science of pleasure. The French Laundry serves only small plates because, according to founder and head chef Thomas Keller, a dish only pleases the palate for the first three or four bites. After that, you are just filling up instead of experiencing ecstasy. So the famous California wine-country establishment triggers your joy over and over by sending lots of tiny new dishes to your table. It's very expensive because of all the labor involved. I haven't been there myself. I decided that I would get more pleasure by spending that amount of money on a lot of cheaper meals.

What if you went to the French Laundry and fell in love with one particular dish? Imagine that you persuaded the chef to make you a full plate of it. When it comes, you dive in with excitement. But after a few bites, you're disappointed. You wonder if they messed up. Maybe they did something different? It's hard to believe that you're perceiving it differently. We are not aware of our own habituation.

The brain triggers joy when it encounters any new way to meet its needs. New food. New love. New places. New techniques. After a while, the new thing doesn't measure up. "It's not the way I remember it." You may wish you could trade it in for another new thing. But when you understand your own brain, you realize that the disappointment comes from you rather than the thing itself.

When a dopamine spurt ends, it may feel like something is wrong. But dopamine is supposed to rise and fall. Imagine your ancestor finding a river full of fish. He's very excited as he runs back to tell his clan about it. Dopamine creates the energy to run back and the memory to find the spot again. Then the dopamine has done its job. It's not needed anymore. He might feel happiness in other ways. Serotonin might surge when he thinks of the respect he will get from his tribe, and oxytocin might spurt when he thinks of the shared pleasure of feasting. But his dopamine will dip unless he finds an even bigger run of fish.

When dopamine dips, your unhappy chemicals get your attention. You get that "do something" feeling, and you have to decide what to do. One option is to accept the unhappy chemicals and figure out what's triggering them. Another option is to quickly distract yourself from them with a behavior you expect to trigger more dopamine.

Imagine a teenager at a gambling casino. He wins $50, and gets extremely excited. His brain "learns" that gambling triggers that great "I did it!" feeling. He is not consciously telling himself that gambling promotes survival. But the next time he feels bad, the idea of going to a casino lights up. When an evening of gambling doesn't trigger the great feeling he expects, he gambles more. Soon he's feeling bad about all the money he lost. The bad feeling drives him to look for a way to feel better, which activates the thought of gambling. You can have a gambling habit at any age. But a young brain more easily builds neural highways big enough to endure despite disappointment.

When you're young, it's easy to experience something as "the best ever" and "the worst ever." Your brain sees this as important survival information, so your neurochemicals are triggered. That "paves" neural pathways, which help recognize that experience in the future. Of course when you encounter it again, it is no longer the best or worst you've ever experienced.

Imagine a child winning a spelling bee. He feels more respect and acceptance (serotonin and oxytocin) than ever. He wants that good feeling again, so he spends a lot of time studying spelling words. His brain squirts dopamine each time he mentally seeks and finds the spelling of a word. Every step toward his goal triggers more dopamine. The good feeling distracts him from any bad feelings he may have had. You can't control many of the threats around you, so it's nice to know you can get a good feeling whenever you pick up your dictionary. It works if your brain has linked spelling to an anticipated reward.

But the day will come when this habit disappoints. If the child wins a few more competitions, the same old reward may fail to mask the threatened feelings he is experiencing. He will seek a bigger reward to trigger more dopamine. He might focus on the school talent show, or getting into Harvard.

Whether you've linked dopamine to studying or gambling, it eventually disappoints. Like the juiced-up monkeys in Chapter 1, your brain takes the juice you have for granted instead of cranking out more happy chemicals. But if you lose the juice you took for granted, you're darned unhappy. Managing such a brain is not easy, but it's the responsibility that comes with being alive.

Drug addicts say they are "always chasing the first high." The first time you take a drug, the good feeling is more intense than any feeling you could get naturally. Since your brain equates good feelings with meeting your survival needs, it seems like the drug meets your needs better than anything you've ever experienced. You take the drug again, expecting more of that feeling. But this time it is not the best feeling you've ever had. You're disappointed. If you took more, that could be the best experience ever....You are constantly choosing between disappointment and taking more.

Your brain is chasing the first high whether it's a natural or an artificial high you're anticipating. Artificial highs build bigger circuits and usually have worse side effects, but many natural-high stimulators have harmful side effects when repeated too often. People keep seeking despite the side effects because the expectation of a reward equals dopamine. Whether you are seeking the next drink or the next donut or the next shopping expedition or the next investment, your dopamine starts flowing the moment you start seeking it. The reward is never as big as you expect, so you continue seeking.

We don't usually think of seeking as fun. When you seek a donut, you think it's the donut you want. But that great dopamine feeling flows while you're looking for a parking spot near the donut shop. To your brain, it's like foraging: scanning the environment for details leading to a reward. When you find a parking spot, your brain says hooray! More dopamine. We evolved to survive by sifting through lots of detail in search of reward-relevant patterns. Whether you're looking for a good bar, or a good stock, or a good gift, seeking stimulates dopamine.

Computer games reward that urge to seek and find, but not if you play the same game over and over. That's why you get rewarded with a new level. Going to a museum or a mall stimulates dopamine because you are busy scanning lots of details in search of familiar patterns. It's foraging without the food. But you need to keep scanning new details or your dopamine will droop. That's why museums change their exhibitions and malls change their merchandise.

When a game or museum or mall stops feeling good, you might say "they don't make them like they used to." You may not realize that the change is in you rather than in the outside world. When your brain can find a reward without much seeking, it doesn't release much dopamine.

Dopamine disappointments	

Collecting is a popular hobby because it overcomes dopamine disappointment. It gives you a never-ending reason to seek. As soon as you find one object of desire, you look for another. You always know what you "need" because the collection defines it. You bring lots of knowledge to the pursuit, so your mind is too busy to notice unhappy chemicals.

Adding to your collection feels like meeting a survival need, even though nothing you collect actually promotes survival. You rarely hear a collector say their collection is complete and they are just enjoying it as is. The good dopamine feeling stops if you stop seeking. Collecting also stimulates oxytocin and serotonin as you bond with and one-up other collectors.

Planning a project triggers dopamine. It might be a party or a home re-model or a life transition. Thinking about the end result makes you feel good, and each step that brings you closer stimulates dopamine despite the inevitable frustration of a long-term project. Once the party is over or the house is remodeled, you may feel like something is missing. Dopamine is missing, and you may be tempted to start a new project.

Travel stimulates dopamine because it bombards your senses with new inputs. Planning a trip stimulates it too because you anticipate the great feeling of being at your destination. When you arrive at that tropical island with its perfect bands of blue and white, you get a rush of excitement. But in a few minutes your focus shifts to the practicalities of settling into your room, and the dopamine wears down. When you wake up the next morning, the excitement of being there is somewhat fresh again. But as the day wears on, you become who you were before the vacation.

Not all dopamine-fueled habits are bad habits. Thomas Edison stayed up late at night trying again and again to find filaments that would make electric light. Diseases have been cured because researchers spent long hours sifting and sorting through details in search of patterns. When they found what they were looking for, they typically set out in search of the next goal. Our brains were not designed for us to sit around contemplating what we already have. They were not designed to trigger excitement for no reason. They were designed for us to keep finding new ways to promote survival.

Romantic love is perhaps the most familiar example of dopamine disappointment. When people are "in love," they don't realize they are riding on the dopamine triggered by the satisfaction of a long quest or pursuit. The same reward does not excite you forever. Dopamine dips, and unhappy chemicals get your attention. You may think your partner is causing the unhappiness because you don't understand dopamine disappointment. You may think a new partner will make you happy, because your brain learned that from the last partner. But if you expect to feel the excitement of new love all the time, you will probably find yourself in a vicious cycle.

If you expect a life of constant dopamine joy and excitement, you are likely to be disappointed.

Endorphin Disappointment

Real pain triggers endorphin. But if you took the drastic step of inflicting pain on yourself to get the endorphin, you would be disappointed. It would take more and more pain to trigger the same endorphin feeling.

Starving yourself stimulates a good endorphin feeling, but you have to keep starving more to get the same feeling.

Exercise triggers the good feeling, but the same level of exertion will soon disappoint you. You have to keep doing more to get the same feeling.

Obviously, hurting your body to enjoy the endorphin is a tragic and dangerous vicious cycle. But it explains why people who hurt themselves seem inclined to hurt themselves more. We did not evolve to inflict pain on ourselves intentionally to get an endorphin high. Pain warns you of imminent survival threat. In the world before emergency rooms and anesthesia, the bad feeling was incentive enough to avoid pain-inflicting behaviors.

If you are a person who never exercises, you will get a great endorphin feeling the first day you start. That's a nice reward, and of course you should continue to exercise. But you won't get that good feeling the second day unless you exercise more. And of course, you should. However, the day will soon come when one of your body parts cannot tolerate the escalation necessary for endorphin. If you can't get yourself to exercise without that reward, you're in trouble.

Some people are so intent on endorphin that they harm their body until they get it. I used to play tennis in a friendly, uncompetitive ladies group. I was amazed to learn that most of the ladies played in pain. Many of them took anti-inflammatories before they went out to play. My father died of liver cancer after taking these pain relievers, so I quit the tennis group and looked for other kinds of exercise. When I run into the tennis ladies, they look good, but when I ask how they feel, they are still in pain.

Starving triggers endorphin. If you ever missed a couple of meals, you may have started feeling a little high. As soon as you eat something, that good feeling stops. Your body knows that the good feeling of eating has more survival value than the good feeling of starving. The pain of starving is survival information we were not designed to ignore.

Opium and its derivatives stimulate endorphin without physical pain. But they have terrible side effects. First, they undermine your natural happy-chemical mechanism. Second, they mask any pain you have while using them, resulting in dangerous neglect of personal care. Third, you habituate to them, so you need to use more to get the same effect. Harmful side effects accumulate quickly, leading to more unhappy chemicals, more urge to use, and a fast-spinning vicious cycle.

Endorphin disappoints you after a short time because it evolved for emergency use only. But endorphin masks social pain so well that people are tempted to endure physical pain to get more of it. Tragically, the body habituates to the pain but the brain keeps seeking the good feeling. When you try to manipulate your body into triggering endorphin, you can do damage without noticing.

Endorphin disappointments	😐

Oxytocin Disappointment

A good way to understand oxytocin disappointment is to imagine yourself getting a massage. The first few moments feel phenomenal. Then your mind drifts and you can literally forget you are receiving a massage. You enjoy it, of course, but the oxytocin explosion doesn't last. You might blame your massage therapist if you don't understand that your brain habituates to things, even great things.

Oxytocin is released at birth, which eases the stress of coming into the world. But soon you need more. Animals lick their young and humans cuddle them. As oxytocin is stimulated, the child learns to trust the parent. That wires the child to trigger oxytocin in future circumstances that are similar.

When our trust is disappointed, we wire ourselves to fear trusting in future circumstances that are similar. Social trust is not easy to sustain. We mammals are so alert for potential threats that you may feel attacked when you hear a slight change in tone. Oxytocin protects you from quitting your job the moment a co-worker wrinkles his forehead at you, or running away from home the moment your relatives cluck their tongues at you. Oxytocin protected your ancestors from leaving the tribe every time someone got on their nerves, thus saving them from the dangers that befall lone individuals in the wilderness. But at some point, your bad feelings about someone exceed your good feelings, and you lose trust.

Children on a playground learn about social trust. They learn to seek support where good feelings are triggered, and not to expect support where cortisol has been triggered. If a classmate helps you with homework, it feels good and a path to your oxytocin is paved. When a schoolmate disappoints you, the bad feelings make connections that protect you from more bad feelings.

The pain of disappointed trust enters every life. If your parents put your needs first when you were young, it's disappointing to learn that the rest of the world doesn't treat you this way. And if your parents were not worthy of your trust, then you learned about disappointment even earlier.

Whether or not you suffer the kind of dramatic betrayals well-known in fiction, smaller disappointments of trust are part of daily life. For example, you may feel disillusioned when you're finally accepted into a group or organization you longed to be in. Before you were admitted, you idealized the group. You imagined how good it would feel to belong. But once you're in it, you see its flaws. You wonder how they could be so crass. You start thinking that maybe another group or organization would make you happy. A vicious cycle can result.

Gangs are a tragic example of oxytocin disappointment. People join gangs because they create a sense of security and protection. Social trust develops through aggression against rival gangs. But group mates also turn on each other as they jockey for position within the group. The risk is huge in a culture of aggression, since those closest to you can most easily harm you. The risk motivates gang members to build solidarity through more aggression against third parties. They're in a vicious cycle.

My grandparents came from Sicily, where the Mafia builds social bonds with violence. The Mafia offers the illusion of safety by promising protection from violence if you cooperate. But you're not safe for long because one day you will inconvenience the predators you associate with and become prey rather than an ally. You learn that you cannot trust anyone. This dangerous isolation leaves you eager to trust anyone who triggers your oxytocin with a gesture of goodwill, and the cycle continues.

No one mentioned the Mafia when I was growing up, and I presumed it was an invention of Hollywood. But I began researching my roots and was horrified to discover the tragic lives of my ancestors. Surviving in a culture of violence means choosing at every moment between the risk of cooperating and the risk of not cooperating. Trust sounds like a virtue, but trusting a predator who expects complete submission may not promote survival. Or it may. The uncertainty is huge.

All human cultures experience oxytocin disappointment in some way. Primates build in-group bonds by distinguishing themselves from out-groups. But within the group, conflict is a routine part of primate life. Group members tolerate the pain because they don't want to lose their social support network. They accept behaviors from group-mates that they would never tolerate from outsiders. A big part of social trust is sustaining expectations despite disappointments. That's what oxytocin circuits do.

"Battered spouse syndrome" is a tragic example of oxytocin disappointment, as is "battered child syndrome." Abused individuals often cover up for their abusers instead of promoting their own survival. They blame themselves for the betrayal of trust and desperately seek ways to re-kindle it. Instead of building new trust with new people, they keep trying to build it with the abuser they're wired to expect good feelings from.

An alcoholic looking for someone to drink with is another famous example of oxytocin disappointment. People seek trust from those they expect to accept them, bad habits and all. Eaters bond with eaters, drug users bond with drug users, shoppers bond with shoppers and angry ragers bond with angry ragers. When you're with your social allies, you can feel good about yourself despite your drinking or shopping or raging. But when you decide to get control of your habit, you will not get support from your allies. They may even undermine your efforts to conquer your habit. Many people continue the habit rather than risk losing their friends. When the habit makes them feel bad, their "friends" make them feel good.

Trust is nice, but too much trust can undermine survival. Imagine a child who trusts his parents to tie his shoes and cut his meat for too long. Imagine a student who trusts others to do his homework for him. Imagine a spouse who trusts his partner to deal with the world for him. The good feeling of trust may distract you from building the skills you need to promote your own survival. Awareness of your limitations gives you a bad feeling, so you quickly seek a good feeling by leaning on the person you trust. More frustration results, and your brain does something about it in the way it has learned. A vicious cycle of trust and frustration results.

Oxytocin disappointments	

If you expect the good feeling of oxytocin to bring you constant happiness and relieve all your unhappy chemicals, you are likely to be disappointed.

Serotonin Disappointment

When people respect you, it feels good, and your brain looks for ways to get that feeling again. But the same old respect doesn't thrill you after a while, and your brain looks for ways to get more. When your quest for respect is disappointed, it feels bad. You look for a way to feel good, and getting more respect is one way your brain knows to do that.

When you go to a shop or a restaurant, the staff treats you with great respect. They're paid to act like the customer is always right. But you don't get such deference in the rest of life. Most of the time, you live in a world where others are as convinced of their cause as you are of yours. If you rely too much on the pleasure of getting respect, you may end up disappointed.

When we see others caught in this conundrum, we may think they are foolish. We know our survival does not depend on which table we sit at for lunch. But the brain evolved to keep striving to promote itself. It did not evolve to say, "I'm important enough now. I can just relax."

Every Hollywood story has this thread. No matter how much recognition a person gets, they feel bad when it stops. They blame others for their loss of the limelight (the ruthlessness of the industry, the fickleness of public taste, the incompetence of management). They don't blame their own mammal brain, which refuses to release more serotonin unless you get more respect. While it's easy to notice this theme in the movies, it pervades private life too. Getting respect from those around you feels good, and some people don't know when to stop. They make a habit of imposing their wishes on others just for the pleasure of it. As soon as that pleasure ebbs, they have an urge to do it again. When they lack a way to get deference from others and have to face the world without that serotonin boost, they crash and burn.

Paradoxically, the quest for respect has also fueled human achievement. The desire for respect is real; squelching it is no path to happiness. But to seek respect is to risk disappointment. Serotonin inevitably dips because you cannot get increasing respect every moment of your life. When it dips, you might get the feeling that something is wrong with the world. You might rush to seek more, and ignore the side effects.

A person who buys the latest status object feels frustrated when others catch up. A person who gets their dream job soon focuses on the next dream job. A person who controls every move of those around him complains that his subordinates don't comply fast enough. A big fish in a small pond dreams of a bigger pond.

You may think you'll be happy once you set a record at your bowling alley, but your mind will soon turn to the next record. The brain learns to feel important in a particular way, and then it looks for more of that feeling.

When Marlon Brando wails, "I coulda been a contender," in *On the Waterfront*, you believe he'd be happy if he had won a boxing title. But in all probability, his brain would have contended for more once he got it.

Many people stimulate that good serotonin feeling by trying to rescue others. Feeling like a hero is a reliable way to stimulate your serotonin. But the good feeling soon passes and you have to rescue again. Sometimes rescuers reward bad behavior in others because they are so eager to rescue. Some rescue efforts fail, and the rescuer urgently seeks any rescue opportunity they can find because that's how their brain learned to shift from bad feelings to good feelings.

Serotonin disappointment is often blamed on "our society," but status-seeking is easy to see in other cultures and time periods. In traditional cultures, mothers-in-law often dominate their daughters-in-law with sheer despotism. Cruelty to servants is often accepted. We may think tribal societies are egalitarian when their dominance hierarchy is implicit. But unspoken expectations are often backed up by violence, so each individual quickly submits to avoid harm. Traditional people, like modern people, live in cultures that do not give them a serotonin high all the time.

Social dominance commands our attention because it promotes your genes, and that's what mammals care about once their immediate needs are met. This urge is expressed in diverse ways. Many people are interested in helping children get ahead. And many people are interested in how their hair looks. You may not be focused on reproduction per se, but anything that could affect your reproductive potential triggers your brain chemicals. That's why "bad hair" and children's disappointments trigger surprisingly bad feelings. Any small obstacle to getting respect can trigger you more than you might have thought.

People often have a sense of crisis today, though our lives are far more secure than our ancestors. That's because your brain doesn't compare your life to your ancestors' lives. It compares with something you know, like the cousin who is doing better than you. No matter how much good you have, that cousin is a reminder of what you don't have. Perhaps you grew up hearing a parent complain about what others got that they didn't get. Instead of enjoying your freedom from the constant disease and violence of the past, your brain looks for more, and gets disappointed.

When you see others get recognition you long for, it can feel bad. Your brain looks for ways to feel better, and what it comes up with is anything that got you recognition in the past. If you don't get the recognition you seek, you try again. When children fail to make the team or get a prom date, we teach them to keep trying. Seeking recognition is part of a healthy human life, despite the potential for disappointment. Animals often stop trying because they get bitten and clawed when they over-reach. But humans are polite to the telemarketer and the failed election candidate and the washed-up singer. We know they are seeking happiness in whatever way they've learned.

Winning the love of a higher-status person is a widespread strategy for stimulating serotonin. Of course, we don't consciously equate love with status. But when a high-status person of the right gender notices you, your brain lights up. Your neurochemistry screams *"Go toward this. It is very good for your survival."* Even bonobos, the apes known for their sexual dynamism, compete vigorously for high-status partners.

Once that trophy partner is yours, however, your serotonin stops surging. It would surge again if you found an even higher-status love object. Probably you restrain the urge to do that, but you can imagine others yielding to it. A super-star spouse makes a person feel good, and that wires the brain to expect good feelings by acquiring a super-star spouse again. That is why some people repeat the quest despite the side effects.

Many people protect themselves from serotonin disappointment by saying they don't care about status. But their neurochemicals respond to their status ups and downs whether they intend to or not. The response is shaped by life experience. If you lived a few centuries ago, you might have fought duels to defend your status. Females were often confined to their homes to protect their status.

No matter what your experience, the circuits you built when you were young are the superhighways to your neurochemicals. Perhaps you grew up with relatives who dominated you, and you learned to expect disrespect from others. By contrast, you may have grown up with a lot of admirers, and now you expect admiration from others. No matter how you got wired up, respect feels good, but the feeling soon passes and you have to do more to get more.

If you expect serotonin to make you feel good all the time, you will be disappointed.

Serotonin disappointments	

© 2012 L. Breuning

Habits and Side Effects

The curious thing about disappointment is that it doesn't delete the circuit. If you expect a lottery ticket to make you feel good, you keep expecting that after many tickets lose. If you expect a night on the town to make you feel good, you keep expecting that even though you wake up feeling bad and not remembering the night.

We often respond to disappointment by trying again. That means we get the side effects again. At first, side effects are small, so it's easy to tell yourself "it's just one little cookie." "It's just one little drink." "It's just a little flirtation." "It's just a little splurge." "It's just a little anger." "It's just a little down time." "It's just a little risk." "It's just a little party." "It's just a little project." "It's just a little confidence-booster." "It's just a little lie." "It's just a little competition."

Side effects pile up when you repeat a behavior a lot. But you want to repeat it anyway because you expect it to replace unhappy chemicals with happy chemicals. This may not sound logical, but neural pathways are not created by logic. They're created by repetition and emotion, as we'll see in the following chapter.

The quirky "logic" of our neural pathways was explained to me by a hypnotist who helps people quit smoking. Imagine a fourteen year-old boy at a party, he said. The boy sees a girl he wants to talk to, but he's afraid. He tries a cigarette to steady his nerves, and it works! The girl returns his affection, and his happy chemicals flow. His brain connects the cigarette to the reward. And because this reward is so relevant to "reproductive success," it triggers a huge spurt of neurochemicals, creating a huge link in his brain. Cigarettes meet survival needs, from the mammal brain's perspective. Of course the boy doesn't think this in words, but the next time he needs confidence in the face of a "survival challenge," his brain will light up the idea of smoking. The neural pathway keeps developing.

If this person tries to stop smoking years later, the insecurity of the fourteen year-old boy at a party will suddenly well up in him. That insecurity has no where to go without the smoking pathway. Until he builds a new pathway, he will feel like his survival is threatened when he resists the urge for a cigarette. His mammal brain will think of smoking as its survival tool until he gives it a new survival tool.

Without your happy habit, unhappy chemicals can seem overwhelming. It feels like you're in danger, even when you're actually reducing your danger by avoiding harmful behaviors. Your neurochemicals may give you the idea that you must repeat the "happy" behavior now to save your life. But your cortex can inhibit an impulse from the mammal brain. The moment you do that, a virtuous circle begins.

Building a Virtuous Circle

All it takes to start a virtuous circle is to do nothing. That's hard to do in the moment your unhappy chemicals are screaming "do something or you will die." But if you do something, you are likely to repeat the vicious cycle. Doing nothing is the first step to freeing yourself from it.

Doing nothing means accepting unhappy chemicals instead of rushing to fix them or mask them. Then your brain learns that you won't die, even though it feels that way.

Doing nothing gives your brain time to generate an alternative. You may have no alternative that feels as good as you expect your happy habit to feel. But the more you do nothing in the face of that "do something feeling," the more you give alternative pathways a chance to grow. Over time, you will trigger happy chemicals in new ways and your new pathways will grow solid. Eventually, they will steer electricity away from the habit you'd rather do without.

New habits are not easy to develop. A new behavior that feels good instantly is likely to have side effects of its own. A new behavior that doesn't feel good instantly is hard to build into a habit.

But when you know how your brain works, you can build more happy habits with fewer side effects. You can start a virtuous circle without being virtuous. The following chapters show how.

4

How Your Brain Wires Itself

Building new neural circuits is hard because your old pathways are efficient. Flimsy new pathways have trouble competing with them. Here's a brief explanation of how your existing circuits got built from experience. Understanding your equipment makes it easy to see why old circuits have power, and why persistence is needed to build new ones.

Five Ways Experience Changes Your Brain

1. Experience Insulates Your Neural Wiring

The neurons you use repeatedly develop a fatty coating called "myelin." Myelinated neurons are extremely fast, like optical fiber. Most of your myelination occurred by age fifteen, and a lot of it happen by age two. Young brains produce a lot of myelin, which is why child prodigies exist, and why it's hard to learn a new language after puberty. Myelinated circuits make a task feel effortless compared to doing it with slow, naked neurons.

The adult brain is stingy with myelin. We did not evolve to rebuild our neural networks in adulthood. We evolved to build an operating system during our years of dependency, and then start helping children build their operating system.

Myelination requires repetition, even when you're young. Anything you do repeatedly in youth develops big branches in your neural network. Myelinated neurons look white, which is why we have "white matter" under our "gray matter." In a significant way, it's the core of who you are.

You rely on your myelinated circuits most of the time because they're so efficient. When you use neurons you haven't already greased, something feels wrong. It's the feeling you have when you try to speak a foreign language. Your thoughts come faster than your words because they're produced by myelinated circuits while the words come from scrawny, undeveloped circuits. Perhaps you've gone skiing and watched a tiny kid whiz past you. You struggle to execute a checklist of bodily movements you learned in a lesson, while the child seems to do it effortlessly.

You may think myelin is "wasted" on the young. But in the state of nature, it makes sense to build a mental model of the world when you're young and then stick with it. Once you learn that fire is hot and gravity makes you fall, and you don't need to re-learn it. At puberty you need to update your mental model of the world as you move to a new ecological niche to improve your reproductive prospects. That's why myelin spurts around puberty. After that, creatures put their neural network to use forming the next generation instead of re-inventing the wheel. As much as you might prefer to unlearn some things you learned long ago, it's good to know why your brain doesn't cooperate.

2. Neurons Atrophy from Lack of Experience

Your brain started pruning itself at age two. Neurons that weren't used began to wither. Surprisingly, this stimulates knowledge. It helps a toddler use the circuits he's already built instead of spreading his attention around the way a newborn does. A toddler focuses on things that felt good or bad to him in the past, and those circuits build.

The brain does much of its pruning between ages two and seven. This helps a child to link new learning to his existing circuits instead of building lots of separate circuits. Richly interconnected networks are much more useful in making sense of the world.

By the time you are seven, you are good at seeing what you have already seen and hearing what you have already heard. You may think this is bad, but the value is clear if you think about how easy it is to lie to a six-year old. Tell the same lie to an eight-year old and he will question it. He compares what you tell him to his life experience. If there's no fit, he's able to trust his own mental representation of the world instead of yours. This had tremendous survival value in a world where parents often died young and children met their own survival needs.

When you were young, some of your neurons were swept away like autumn leaves, which streamlined your thought process. You kept adding new knowledge, of course. But you focused on things relevant to your old knowledge. You tended to shy away from things completely unconnected to your past experience, because they were hard to process. When electricity speeds through your circuits, you have the feeling you know what is going on. When you see things unrelated to your prior experience, little electricity is triggered, so you have little confidence in your information.

Unfamiliar inputs are not connected to your neurochemicals, so it's hard to judge if they're "good for you" or "bad for you." Your brain is motivated to see the good and avoid the bad, so it focuses on inputs relevant to those goals. As a result, you keep developing connected neurons and not developing others. Some neurons atrophy because they haven't become relevant to your survival.

3. Experience Makes Synapses Efficient

Electricity does not flow easily through your brain. When an electrical impulse travels along a neuron, it dies out when it reaches the end unless it has enough oomph to jump across the gap, or *synapse* to the next neuron. Synapses that haven't been crossed before are inefficient and harder to cross. But electricity sails easily across a developed synapse, so one neuron reliably activates the next.

Synapses develop from repetition and emotion. Emotions develop a synapse quickly, while repetition develops them slowly.

Emotions are neurochemicals that make immediate and permanent changes to the synapses they encounter. Here's a simple example. I used to carry popcorn on long plane trips because it was a convenient and welcome pleasure. One day I chipped a tooth on popcorn, and I never wanted to travel with it again. In an instant, the feeling of being stranded in the air with a cracked tooth triggered enough cortisol to build a strong new connection.

Repetition can develop a synapse without neurochemicals, but it takes a lot longer. When a synapse is activated many times, it gradually becomes efficient at transmitting an electrochemical signal.

Synapses are not like muscles in the sense that we need to develop all of our muscles, but if you developed all your synapses you couldn't make sense of the world. Instead, we develop networks that represent our environment, so we can sift down to the facts most relevant to survival. We are intelligent because our neurons are connected in ways that reflect our good and bad experiences with the world around us. Synapses create the connections, whether they build up slowly from repetition or get turbo-charged by molecules of pleasure or pain.

4. New Synapses Grow

Each neuron can have many synapses because it can grow multiple branches or *dendrites*. New dendrites and synapses get created because two neurons literally reach out and touch each other if they are stimulated at the same time. A neuron grows toward an electrical hot spot, and a new synapse is born when a dendrite gets close enough for its electricity to jump to another neuron. When this happens, you connect two ideas.

Other people's connections are easy to see. A person who likes politics seems to connect everything to politics. A person who likes dogs connects everything to dogs, and a religious person connects everything to their beliefs. You see one person zooming in on the negative side of things while another sees the positive. When it comes to your own connections, however, it feels like you're just seeing "the truth." You don't realize that your well-used neurons grew tentacles to each other.

5. Emotional Receptors Grow and Atrophy

Neurochemicals are protein molecules that fit receptors on the surface of your neurons. These molecules have complex shapes, so each one fits a specific receptor like a key fits a lock. Sometimes you get flooded by more emotional chemicals than your receptors can process. You feel overwhelmed and disoriented, whether the flood is happy or unhappy. Your brain adapts when you are "going through" something by building more receptors to help you process the messages.

When receptors aren't used for a while, they disappear. This flexibility is good, but it also means that you have to use your happy receptors or lose them.

Happy chemicals float around until they find receptors they can fit into. When a happy-chemical key opens a receptor lock, the neuron fires. That's how you "know" what you're happy about. And that's how you build the expectation of more happiness from a particular source.

Free Will

Neurochemicals are constantly sending signals through your brain and body, but you don't have to act on these signals. Your pre-frontal cortex is able to *inhibit* an action. It's able to shift your attention in one direction or another. That gives your limbic system time to generate a new conclusion about your best survival option.

No matter what circuits you happen to have, you are free to resist an impulse and generate another one. You are constantly deciding whether to act on your impulses or generate alternatives, but you do it so efficiently that you hardly notice.

103

You are free to choose where to direct your attention. You are always deciding which external signals and internal signals to focus on. You are always ignoring some external and internal information because it's impossible to process everything. As the world filters in through your senses and lights up your circuits, you are always choosing whether to act on that impulse or allow the electricity to spill over into another circuit.

Sometimes it feels like a signal has commanded your attention. A signal that fits one of your well-developed circuits activates a strong message effortlessly. A signal that doesn't fit one of your well-developed circuits only gives you a weak message unless you concentrate your attention on it. Your decisions about where to put your attention are the core of your free will. Whether you give your attention to the circuits that surge effortlessly, or concentrate on weaker, more diffuse activations, you are exercising your free will.

Everyone's attention is limited, and the more you invest in one place, the less you have left for other things. The more attention you pay to unfamiliar signals, the less you have left for everything else. You are always deciding which use of your attention best promotes your survival. We guide these decisions with habits so we don't use up our attention on them.

Imagine your ancestor seeing a lion while out hunting. He monitors the lion to see which way it's headed. At some point he decides he's better off running away, and focuses his attention on the ground in front of him instead of the details of the lion. You do the same thing when changing lanes in traffic. From moment to moment, you decide where is the best place to focus your attention in order to be safe. These decisions happen instantaneously so as not to waste your attention.

Now imagine a person who spends most of his attention watching television. When he thinks of shutting the television, he gets a bad feeling. To avoid that threatened feeling, he shifts his attention back to the television. This is his habit, but he is always free to observe other information about what is going on in his life.

Sometimes your brain generates conflicting impulses. You want to smoke and you don't. You want to eat pizza and you don't. You want to study and you don't. You want to call your mother and you don't. You are always deciding which impulse to act on and which to inhibit.

Apes can inhibit an impulse, too. When an ape looks at a juicy mango, he wants it, but he also wants to avoid being bitten by the bigger ape next to him. He inhibits his impulse to grab while assessing all the survival-relevant information around him.

You have more neurons than an ape, especially in the important pre-frontal cortex. You can consider more options, and you can even generate options in your mind that you've never experienced in the sensory world. It all depends on where you direct your attention. When you don't direct, your big old circuits dominate your attention.

Repetition and Emotion Build Connections

Before there was "education," and even before there was language, circuits built from repetition and emotion.

A baby chimpanzee learns while watching the world from his mother's lap. Though he doesn't know what food is, he sees crumbs fall from her mouth. They land on her chest right in front of his eyes. He thinks of grasping a crumb and putting it into his mouth because his mirror neurons light up when she does this. He can't get his muscles to do it until he's made several tries. That's frustrating, but he's fully nourished by her milk and protected by her touch. When he finally gets a crumb into his mouth, it tastes good! His dopamine surges. That feels good, which motivates him to seek more.

Mother chimps don't feed their children except for breast milk. If the little tyke wants solids, he has to get it himself. By the time he's big enough to need the extra nutrition, he has accumulated experience with things you put in your mouth. As he grows, he follows his mother when she forages. He repeatedly sees the plants she chooses. She doesn't explicitly show him or push him. He learns because food is rewarding. Over time, he imitates his mother's foraging behavior and wires himself to eat what she eats. By the time his mother has passed on, he will have the skills he needs to survive without her.

Chimpanzees eat a lot of leaves, and research suggests they can recognize more than a hundred different kinds. They even select leaves with medical properties when they are sick. But the big reward in a chimp's life is food rich in protein, such as nuts, insects and meat. These foods are difficult to obtain. Here again, children are not "provisioned." They only get the reward if they execute the skill.

A young chimp can take years to succeed at cracking open a nut. He gets interested because he tastes the crumbs his mother leaves in the shells of her nuts. "Wow!" His dopamine responds because nuts have a higher fat content than most food he encounters. But when he tries to imitate his mother's nut-cracking movements, the darned thing doesn't open. He persists because the expectation of a big reward triggers dopamine, and because he has other nut-seekers to mirror.

I once spent ten minutes watching a young capuchin monkey try and fail to crack open a nut. I was overwhelmed by an urge to "help," so I looked for a zookeeper. When I found one, she told me they are well fed, and the activity is natural, and I shouldn't worry about it. If I were running that monkey's "education," he wouldn't learn survival skills, and the species would die out.

Young primates learn social skills the same way they learn foraging skills. They start on mother's lap, watching her interact with others. A young monkey sees his mother dominate some of the time and submit some of the time. He doesn't need to label it. His mirror neurons trigger trust when she trusts another, and fear when she fears another. This builds pathways that guide him as he interacts with others directly. He seeks the good feelings of trust and dominance, and avoids the bad feeling of pain. By the time he's grown, he's wired to survive within the social expectations of his troop.

Chimps are not born pre-programmed with all the necessary survival knowledge. We know this because their mothers invest almost five years in them before reproducing again. That means the mother's genetic survival benefits more from nurturing one than from creating another.

Apes learn how to survive from the good feelings of dopamine, oxytocin and serotonin. We do the same. Though we learn some things consciously, like long division and punctuation, we learn a lot from the links our neurochemicals build. Experience tells you whether math or grammar feels good or bad. Mastering something feels good. Being wrong feels bad.

Repetition and emotion work together to build our survival knowledge.

Early survival circuits shape the passions of our lives. Sometimes this is obvious, like a child who decides to be a doctor after watching a sick family member get cured. More often, our passions have no obvious link to survival because a child's understanding of survival is limited. For example, if you got respect from your basket-weaving teacher, you might decide to devote your life to basket-weaving. If you see a rock star getting respect, you might aim to be a rock star. Later on you might realize that your passions do not promote survival, but by then the major pathways to your happy chemicals are already built.

People often complain that "we don't learn from experience." But in fact we do. We learn from experiences that are repeated or neurochemically reinforced. We learn in youth when the brain is more plastic. Experience makes some circuits so efficient that we keep using them. If you have a circuit that gets you into trouble, you can be sure that circuit got you rewards in the past.

Happy-chemical infrastructure

By the time you reach adulthood, you have built the neural infrastructure that tells your brain what is good for you. This is not the survival system you'd come up with if you started today with a blank sheet of paper. It's the system you connected one neuron at a time from the moment your senses began taking in information.

Genes play a role in your neural infrastructure. An amazing example is the laboratory mouse who started digging the first time he touched dirt. His ancestors had lived in cages for 30-60 generations, but when he hit the ground, he dug burrows with characteristics that matched his wild counterparts. The circuits for this survival behavior seem to be inborn.

But our brains are different from mice. Their cortex is tiny, which means their ability to learn from experience is tiny. They are built to run on innate rather than learned circuits. Our cortex is huge because we are designed to fill it up with acquired knowledge. We are not meant to run on pre-loaded programs.

Every creature in nature runs on as few neurons as possible because neurons are metabolically expensive. They consume more oxygen and glucose than an active muscle. It takes so much energy to keep a neuron alive that they actually make it harder to survive. Neurons only promote survival if you really get your money's worth out of them, by wiring them up with survival-relevant information. Natural selection gave humans a gargantuan number of neurons. That means we were meant to use the experience we've stored in our neurons, not to ignore it.

The bigger a creature's cortex, the longer its childhood. It takes a long time to connect neurons in ways that promote survival. Small-brained creatures have short childhoods because they don't need to boot up their operating system. A mouse is a parent by the time it's two months old. A giraffe virtually "hits the ground running." It crashes four feet from the womb to the ground, and in a few weeks it can do almost everything an adult can do. Primates have a very long childhood, by comparison. A monkey's childhood is twice as long as a gazelle's, an ape's childhood is twice as long as a monkey's, and a human's is double that of an ape.

Childhood is metabolically expensive because dependency reduces the number of offspring a mother can have. You might expect natural selection to reward shorter childhoods, but creatures evolved longer childhoods over time. Natural selection rewarded creatures that use their early dependency to learn survival skills.

A long childhood frees a creature from immediate survival pressure so it can learn by interacting with its environment. Animals with short periods of early dependency rely on the survival knowledge they inherited. They're born adapted to a specific ecological niche, and typically die outside that niche. Humans are born ready to adapt to whatever niche we're born into.

And this is why it's so hard to unlearn a happy-chemical strategy once you've learned it. You evolved to rely on your neural network as if your life depended on it.

We don't usually think of our childhood experience as survival knowledge because it doesn't tell you how to get a job with a retirement package. Your early survival learning tells you how to feel good and avoid feeling bad. This is the navigation system you have to pilot yourself through adult survival challenges. For example, your boss makes you feel bad, but the money feels good, and unemployment feels bad, so reconciling with your boss feels good.

Sophisticated adults don't imagine themselves relying on childhood experience to navigate survival. But if you examine your likes and dislikes, you will see how they were built. I discovered a curious example in myself. I noticed that I get excited about opportunities to choose colors. This is not an obvious survival skill, so I tried to make sense of it. The core experience was clear. When I was twelve, my mother inherited $2,000 (about $15,000 in today's money). It was a lot to my mother, and it came from the father who had abused and abandoned her, so she decided to spend it redecorating. She brought me along on shopping missions, and asked my opinion about color swatches.

My mother didn't respect my opinion very often, so this felt good. The happy chemicals told my brain that this was important survival information. I didn't consciously tell myself "choosing colors is a way to get respect." I didn't need to. The respect simply triggered serotonin, and that connected all the neurons that were active at the moment. I created a connection between color and feeling good without knowing it. I didn't do it for lofty reasons. I did it because it was true in my experience.

Most important, the decorating project made my mother happy. I hardly ever saw her happy, so this was significant information for my brain. My mirror neurons registered her happiness without any need for me to consciously embrace decorating. The good feelings wired me to get more good feeling in this particular way. Of all the ways to feel good in the world, the ways already etched into your neurons are the ones you notice.

My brain was already prepared to respond to color long before this happened. When I was in elementary school, my mother gave me a lot of paint-by-number kits. I also made art by gluing mosaic tiles and colored pebbles onto backboards in the manner popular in the early 1960s. These kits gave me a feeling of accomplishment and helped me focus on something other than the unpleasantness around me. Repetition and emotion trained my brain to sift and sort through colors. Without the intent to seek happiness or promote survival, I built circuits for doing that.

© 2012 L. Breuning

When I grew up and got a place of my own, I enjoyed decorating it. In fact, I was constantly interested in redecorating. After a while, I realized that another remodeling project would not really meet my needs. But I still felt the urge to do it. So instead of acting on that urge, I set out to understand it. I traced one experience to another until the connections made sense.

I like color the way many people like sports. If you grew up around someone who loved sports, you found it easy to build that neural infrastructure. When I understood why color made me happy, I looked at it in a new way. I made good use of the happy-chemical infrastructure I had. When I create a slide presentation, I enjoy adding color. When I get dressed or cook dinner, I enjoy the color. I allow myself to linger over the details I'm wired to enjoy. This activates my happy circuits without needing to redecorate. I use my circuits to meet my current survival needs rather than the needs that first built the links.

My brain connected decorating to survival because it connected my mother to survival. We end up with quirky circuits because we build on the connections we have. When you end up with a behavior that doesn't make sense, you can be sure it made sense at an earlier time. You can't just delete it, but you can substitute a new circuit that makes sense to you today. It won't happen effortlessly the way it did when you were young. But repetition and emotion can make it happen.

Social learning equals survival

In the mammal world, social skills are as relevant to survival as physical skills because they're essential for reproductive success. In-born social skills are key for small-brained creatures, but big-brained mammals learn social skills from repetition and emotion.

In the animal world, male and female reproductive strategies are distinct, but both depend on social skills. A female can only birth a limited number of offspring, and many of them perish before puberty. The survival of her genes depends on her ability to keep her children alive. Social skills help her get protection, nutrition, and better paternal genes. A male mammal has less invested in each offspring, so his genes benefit from a quantity strategy. Social skills help him attract females and compete with other males. The male and female strategies overlap, and evolution seems to increase the overlap.

For both genders, the acceptance and respect of your peers promotes survival. Monkey studies show that social alliances increase mating opportunities and boost the survival prospects of the young. So it's not surprising that natural selection created a brain that seeks social alliances. Social skills build without effort or intent as you interact with the world around you.

Children build social skills without insight into their long-term needs. A child survives by getting social support, and his happy chemicals build links when he gets it. Any behavior that works builds a link, even if it seems anti-social or anti-survival from an adult perspective. If a bad behavior gets a child a reward, his brain tags that behavior as useful for survival. If a child gets a lot of support when they are hostile or aggressive, and the support disappears when they're cooperative, their brain learns to be hostile or aggressive. If a child gets rewarded when they're sick, and they lose the rewards as they get well, those neurochemical ups and downs build lasting links

Your brain doesn't care what parenting experts and etiquette manuals say. It builds links when you actually feel rewarded or threatened. You end up with a complex neural infrastructure for seeking respect, acceptance and trust.

Adolescence added a layer to your infrastructure. The hormones of puberty are neurochemicals that cause your neurons to connect and myelinate more easily. Anything that got you respect or attention in your teen years developed big fat circuits. Any threat to your respect and attention in this period made an impression on your brain. Whatever helped you build trust with social allies, or threatened the trust you had, built your pathways. Whenever you experienced the thrill of new rewards, you built links that remain with you.

The neuroplasticity of puberty helps us build new circuits just when we need them. In nature, adolescents often leave home to reproduce. That prevents in-breeding, which leads to more surviving offspring. Brains good at learning a new environment in puberty had more reproductive success, and natural selection built a brain good at re-building its circuits then.

Social survival circuits	
Early Childhood	
Teen Years	

© 2012 L. Breuning

Social learning interconnects with other learning. Basic physiological functions like walking, eating and even breathing are shaped by social learning. An infant learns to regulate his breathing when he's held against his mother's chest and he feels her breathe. Physical needs and social needs are one to a child.

Children learn self-management by experiencing the way the adults around them manage themselves. You add a layer of self-management circuits in adolescence through interactions with peers and available adults. You didn't choose the early rewards and pains that wove your circuits. And you needn't remember the experiences that built them to be motivated by them today. We are born to build our social operating system in youth.

Remodeling

Most people end up with a circuit they'd rather do without. And most people wish for more happy chemicals with fewer side effects. You can build new circuits, but not in the effortless way it happened the first time. It takes repetition and emotion.

Emotion is a Catch-22 because anything that feels good quickly has side effects. People often gain weight when they quit smoking because food feels good instantly. People often develop a new phobia when they conquer an old phobia because it immediately restores that feeling of control. Emotion works fast, but it leads to behaviors with unwanted consequences.

Repetition takes time, but it builds behaviors with fewer side effects. If you expose yourself to something over and over, it can "grow on you." You can get to like things that are good for you, even if you don't like them instantly. But who wants to repeat something over and over if it doesn't feel good? Usually, people don't, which is why we tend to rely on the circuits built by accidents of experience. You will be shaped by accident unless you start repeating things by choice.

Learning to like something new takes longer than you'd think, however. Your brain doesn't see it as important information if it doesn't trigger your happy chemicals. And new things are hard to focus on because the neurons don't fire easily.

Here's a simple example. Fred wants to drink less alcohol. He decides to substitute a new pleasure with fewer side effects. He looks around for something that can grow on him and remembers how he enjoyed sketching when he was young. He resolves to take out his sketch pad every time he feels like drinking. Fred doesn't actually feel like sketching when he longs for a drink. And once he starts sketching, he doesn't feel fabulous. So he accepts that he will live with bad feelings for a while. He plans to do this for two months because he has a big event on the calendar then.

At first, he finds it hard. He hates his sketches and he hates the feeling he gets when he doesn't drink. But he sticks to his goal of repeating the strategy whether it feels good immediately or not. After a while, Fred learns to see the sketching time as a gift he's given himself rather than an extra burden on his already hard life. He learns that his unhappy feelings pass without killing him, and once they've passed, he discovers the pleasure of being alert and responsible. Before the two months are over, he stops looking at the calendar. His sketching circuit grew big enough to compete with his alcohol circuit. Now, he's a healthy person with a fun hobby and a cool skill, not a person at war with himself.

Choosing an activity already linked to his happy chemicals helped him reach his goal of feeling good without alcohol. Sketching gives Fred something to do when his brain has that "do something" feeling. He needed to build a big circuit to compete with the alcohol circuit that was already big. Fred is so pleased with his re-model that he decides to create another new circuit to tackle another challenge in his life.

Deciding which alternative circuit to build is complex. Sometimes it takes a little trial and error to find a new habit that works and minimizes side effects. Consider Louise, who wants a new job but can't get herself to make a sustained job search. She feels bad about her prospects, so she spends her time on things that help her not think about it. A vicious cycle results. Louise resolves to break the cycle by learning to feel good about job hunting. She sets the goal of applying to two jobs a day, developing her career skills for two hours a day, and then feeling good about the effort.

On the first day, she meets her goal, but feels awful. She rewards herself with an ice cream, but finds herself craving more ice cream when she finishes. The next day, she calls a friend after her accomplishment, but finds she does not enjoy discussing these labors. On the third day, it's dark by the time her career advancement work is over, so she decides to celebrate with a night on the town. The next morning, she finds it hard to get started. She goes to a coffee shop, and by the time she finishes the coffee, she's in the middle of her first application. It flows without pain, so the next day, she heads for a designer coffee, and brims with ideas as she drinks it. The following day, she finds herself actually looking forward to her coffee-plus-accomplishment routine, and by the next week she has figured out how to make low-fat designer drinks at home. When six weeks have gone by, she's under consideration for a number of jobs, and has accumulated a wealth of interview experience. Most important, she feels good about doing it, so she wants to do more.

The point is not that coffee solves problems. The point is that inertia is hard to overcome. A habit that will feel good later can be hard to start now. With trial and error, you can find a new habit that will work for you.

Every brain is different. Some people would have a whole pot of coffee and never push the submit button on those job applications. Some people would sketch passionately but spill wine all over their sketchpad. You might experiment with a few alternatives before you commit to one for 45 days. But if you keep starting over, your new habit will never build. After a few test runs, you must commit to repeating your new behavior whether it feels good or not.

Everyone can find a healthy new behavior and repeat it until it becomes a habit. No one can do this for you and you cannot do it for someone else.

5
Building New Happy Circuits

Investing in New Infrastructure

If you were planning a trip to the Amazon, you'd have to choose between cool places that are far from paved roads and destinations that are reasonably accessible. The exotic locales would entice you, but when you saw what it took to get there, you might gravitate toward the beaten path.

It's the same way with your jungle of neurons. You'd love to try out new trails, but when you see how hard it is to slash through one step at a time, you opt for the well-paved neural highways.

You can pave a new road in your brain in 45 days if you repeat a new behavior every day. You must do it each day without fail so the trail gets established. Otherwise, the undergrowth will grow back and the trail you worked so hard to blaze will disappear. You'd be starting from scratch the next time. But if you spark the trail daily whether you feel like it or not, in 45 days it will feel natural. It may not produce the highs of your old happy habit, but you will free yourself of the lows that habit caused. You will be so pleased with your new highway that you will want to build another, and another.

Here are some suggestions for building new roads to dopamine happiness, endorphin happiness, oxytocin happiness, and serotonin happiness. Following that are road-building strategies for any happy chemical. You will decide which new circuits are right for you, and then build your new roads until they conduct as much traffic as your old ones.

Repeating something that doesn't feel good may be taxing at first. Nibbling on carrot sticks doesn't feel as good as licking ice cream, and it's hard to believe that would change in 45 days. Doing homework doesn't feel as good as watching a movie, and you don't see how can repetition make it any different. If you stick to your plan anyway, carrot sticks and studying will soon be connected to your happy chemicals. You will soon feel good when you do what's good for you.

I stumbled on the power of repetition when I noticed that certain music made me happy. I don't mean music that I actually like. I don't mean music that reminds me of a day at the beach. I mean music that I was exposed to by accident. When I was young, music chosen by my brother, my father, my boss at work, and the cafeteria I ate in were always there in the background. When I hear these songs today, I feel strangely happy, whether or not I liked them at the time.

This mystified me until I read a book called *Flow*, by Csikszentmihalyi. It explained that music gives pleasure because your mind keeps predicting what comes next. Each correct prediction triggers dopamine. Unfamiliar music doesn't trigger dopamine because you don't make good predictions. But music that's too familiar doesn't trigger it either, because you can make the predictions automatically without investing attention. Music makes you happy at the sweet spot in the middle. So any music that makes you happy today will eventually make you less happy because it will become too familiar. If you want to be happy with your music all the time, start exposing yourself to unfamiliar music now, so it will be in the sweet spot by the time you've worn out the old pleasures.

This was a revelation to me. It seemed to explain why happiness is elusive despite our best efforts. And it showed how the counter-intuitive choice to repeat things we don't already enjoy can bring great rewards.

People usually talk about "good music" and "bad music," as if the quality is inherent in the music. We look for good movies and good books, and try to avoid bad ones. But the pleasure we get from these things is shaped by accidents of experience more than we know. You can increase your pleasure if you're willing to do things that don't feel good at first.

No one wants to listen to music they don't like on the assumption that they'll grow to like it. No one wants to befriend a person they don't like or join an activity they're bad at, on the assumption that it will feel good later on. When something feels bad, your brain trusts its own reaction. But you miss out on a universe of potential happiness when you do that.

Your brain treats things you like as if they're special and things you don't like as somehow lacking. You presume there's a good reason for this. When you know that your pathways came from accidents of experience, it's easier to build new ones. And when resisting old paths leaves you feeling like your survival is threatened, it's good to know that feeling is also an accident of experience. With persistence, you can wire yourself to feel good when you do things that are good for you.

Building New Dopamine Circuits

Tell yourself "I did it"

Do a victory dance every day. You score at least one goal each day, so commit to finding it and enjoying it for a moment. You will not conduct a symphony at Carnegie Hall every day. You will not lead starving hordes into the Promised Land every day. Adjust your expectations so you can be pleased with something you actually do. This doesn't mean you are setting your sites low. It doesn't mean you are "full of yourself" or losing touch with reality. It means you linger on your gains the way you already linger on your losses.

Celebrating small steps triggers more dopamine than saving it all up for one big achievement. You will not be celebrating with champagne and caviar each day. You will be giving yourself permission to have that "Touchdown!" feeling. This feeling is better than external rewards. It's free, it has no calories, and it doesn't impair your driving. You have a small victory every day. Why not enjoy it?

Commit to doing this every day, whether it feels good or not. At first, it might feel dumb to look for reasons to pat yourself on the back. And the reasons you come up with might make you uncomfortable. But you can decide to be worthy of your own applause and enjoy the feeling, even if just for a split second. If it feels fake or forced, that's normal, because the old circuits that berate your accomplishments feel normal and true.

Do not undermine your good feeling by apologizing to yourself for the triviality of the accomplishment. Just enjoy the split second of triumph and move on. It's just a spark, but if you do it every day for 45 days, you will be your own best spark plug.

Celebrating small accomplishments is a useful skill because big things come from many small steps. Big accomplishments don't make you happy forever, especially when you're in the habit of linking of happiness to a far-off goal. You can learn to be happy with your progress instead.

Your daily triumph will feel better if it doesn't depend on one-upping someone else. If you limit yourself to winning in ways where another person has to lose, you will end up with side effects. You can celebrate what you are creating instead of just who you are defeating.

Move toward a new goal

Ten minutes a day is enough to feel momentum instead of feeling stuck. You don't need a lot of time or money to move toward your big goal. Just commit to spending ten minutes on it each day. That's not enough to move mountains, but it's enough to get close enough to the mountain to see it accurately. Instead of dreaming about your goal from afar, you'll gather the information you need to make a realistic plan. The goal might change as your information grows. Those ten-minute investments can free you from a fantasy goal that wouldn't work, and set you on the road toward a modest goal that you actually achieve. Your ten-minute efforts can help you define manageable steps instead of waiting for huge leaps.

Spend the time on concrete action, not just fantasizing about quitting your day job. Spend it digging into practical realities. Don't spend it all trying to get help from others– it's not their goal. Do this faithfully for 45 days and you will have the habit of moving forward.

If you think you can't spare ten minutes a day, consider the time you already spend dreaming of what you'd rather be doing. You can use that time to research the necessary steps. You will get a dopamine feeling each day as those steps come into view. You will start expecting that dopamine feeling, and look forward to it. You will learn to feel that it's possible to transform a dream into reality with steady effort.

When your ten minutes is over, go back to living in the present. Do not make a habit of putting all your focus on the future.

Divide an unpleasant task into smaller parts

Everyone has a dreaded task that stands in their way. It could be physical, like the mess in your closet that wastes your time every morning. It could be social, like the trust you'd like to repair with someone before it breaks. Commit to spending ten minutes a day on the dreaded task. You don't need to have a solution when you start, just the willingness to take many small steps.

You may think closets cannot be cleaned out in ten-minute chunks. You may think relationships can't be re-negotiated in small bits. But you may never start if the task looks too big, so go into that closet and pull out one chunk of mess and spend ten minutes sorting it. Spend ten minutes planting goodwill where bad will had been growing. Don't let a day go by without tackling the next chunk, and then appreciate yourself for it. Keep it up for 45 days, and you will be comfortable tackling the annoyances that stand in the way of making your life better. The great dopamine feeling will entice you into doing what needs to be done.

If your dreaded task is miraculously finished in a few days, keep going. Find another painful problem to start on so you continue for 45 days. Then you will be in the habit of facing tough challenges in small increments instead of being intimidated by them. Remember to feel good about what you've done each day. Soon, you'll have the habit of tackling obstacles and feeling rewarded by it.

New dopamine strategies	:)

© 2012 L. Breuning

Keep adjusting the bar

Good feelings flow when the level of challenge you face is "just right." If a basketball hoop were too low, you would get no pleasure from scoring points. If the hoop were so high that you never scored, you wouldn't want to play. People enjoy shooting hoops when there's effort and reward for effort. You can adjust the hoops in your life to you get more of that great dopamine feeling. For 45 days, you can experiment with lowering the bar in areas where you have set yourself impossible goals, and raising the bar in places where you score too easily and feel no reward. For example, if you live on frozen dinners while dreaming of cooking gourmet banquets, define a moderate cooking goal and start your 45 days now.

Building New Endorphin Circuits

Laugh

Laughing stimulates endorphin as it spontaneously convulses your innards. Find what makes you laugh, and make time for it. A big *ha-ha* laugh is necessary to trigger endorphin. Just sneering at people you disdain doesn't do it. Nor does laughing on the outside, although that might prime the pump. It can be hard to find what triggers your laughs, but you can commit to keep sampling comedy until you get your daily laugh.

Laughing seems to involve the release of fear. One common fear is expressing emotions deemed unacceptable. When a comedian expresses such feelings in public and survives, it feels good. Put that good feeling at the top of your priority list for 45 days instead of thinking it's frivolous. Don't give up if it takes a bit of shopping. I often find things "not funny" when others enjoy them, but I have found a local improv troop that always seems hilarious to me. So I make time for it.

Cry

Crying releases endorphin along with the unhappy chemicals because of the physical exertion. I am not saying that crying is a good habit. But most adults habitually squelch the urge to cry, and that creates tension. Un-squelching relieves the tension. A few minutes of crying can relieve a bad feeling that you've squelched for years. You can't cry on cue, nor should you make a goal of crying. But for 45 days, you can give yourself time and space and permission to cry if the urge arises. Whether you cry or not, the important step is to notice the physical sensations in your chest, back, abdomen and throat that you are squelching. This tension will loosen when you pay attention to it. The unpleasantness of the moment will pass and the nice loosening will stay with you.

It bears repeating that habitual crying is not the goal. This daily practice is to notice the muscle tension that results when your crying reflex wars with your don't-be-a-crybaby reflex. For 45 days, you can commit to noticing the tension and stopping to feel it instead of ignoring it. The feeling may be so familiar that it's hard to notice. You could get things started by watching *Mommy Dearest* and *Precious* and *Dr. Zhivago*. Other people's tragedies trigger your mirror neurons, and it may feel safer to release grief connected to a stranger's life than to your own.

Crying is our chief survival skill at birth, but over time we learn that crying can leave us worse off. We learn alternatives, but sometimes you completely run out of alternatives and nothing has worked. Your mammal brain releases a desperate feeling, like a trapped animal. Your cortex can distract you away from this feeling, but your muscles can get stuck in the tension that a trapped animal would use to armor itself. You can wear out your crying/breathing muscles in the same way that any over-used body part wears out. Crying can be physical therapy or even ergonomics for your tensed-up diaphragm.

Exercise differently

Changing your exercise routine is a good way to trigger endorphin. When you repeat the same exercise all the time, you are always activating the same muscles and neglecting the same muscles. If you try to get endorphin from the same old exercise routine, you are likely to over-work a few spots beyond their capacity to repair themselves. You can stimulate endorphin by working different places instead.

Your body has three layers of muscles. When you vary your exercise, you give the neglected, constricted layers more attention. Since they're weak, they have to work harder, so you stimulate real development where it's needed without going overboard on the parts you over-rely on. Chasing an endorphin high is not worth the risk of wearing out a part and needing an unpleasant parts-replacement. Variety is a great alternative. And if you're a person who doesn't exercise at all, everything you do will be something different.

When you start a new type of exercise, you may feel uncoordinated. That's just the point. You are stimulating circuits that are not developed. Instead of worrying about your poor performance in the new activity, give yourself 45 days of acceptance. Then try another variety of exercise for 45 days. Of course, don't work any new part beyond its endurance either.

The choices for exercising differently are limitless, but here are two important options.

Stretch

Endorphin is stimulated when you stretch. Everyone can add stretching to their daily routine because you can do it while you're watching TV, waiting on line, and talking on the phone. Mild stretching brings circulation into constricted areas. Stop before you feel pain. Do not assume that if a little is good, a lot must be better. If you stretch every day for 45 days, you will come to enjoy it so much that you will look forward to doing it every day.

New endorphin strategies	🙂

© 2012 L. Breuning

Stretching is not just about arms and legs. Sample a class, such as yoga, to experience deeper stretches without hurting yourself. The point is not to push harder on the usual spots but to stretch spots you didn't know you had, such as the muscles between your ribs. Don't forget to stretch your toes, fingers and even ears.

Slow movement is a variation on this theme. Tai chi and qi gong are so slow that you may think they're not real exercise. But super-slow movement is more of a workout than it seems. It forces you to use muscles evenly, activating the weaker muscles instead of letting the dominant ones take over. Commit to doing something that doesn't look like "real exercise" for 45 days, and you will feel the difference.

Make exercise fun

Consider switching to a fun exercise for 45 days. An exercise that triggers your happy chemicals helps motivate you toward more vigorous exertion. There are endless ways to make exercise fun. I took a waltzing class and was amazed at how hard I worked. Many people make exercise a social activity, from team sports to chatty hikes. It's fun to exercise with music or an enjoyable audio book. Novelty also makes things fun. My yoga teacher makes the class completely different every week. Biking or hiking to new destinations is stimulating. Finally, gardening has an extrinsic reward, which motivates many people to keep exerting. Adding fun to exercise can help you persist.

Building New Oxytocin Circuits

Build on "proxy" trust

Social trust is hard to create, so people often use proxies. Animals, crowds, and digital friends can stimulate the good feeling of social trust without the complications of human bonds. However, these proxies stimulate less oxytocin than live personal contacts. You can get more oxytocin by using these proxies as foundations on which to build.

Proxy trust is comfortable because there's less risk of disappointment. Animals don't betray you, large crowds don't judge you, and digital friends are always available. Direct human trust always comes with the risk of disappointed expectations and feelings of betrayal. Those bad feelings build links that fire when you think about trusting someone. And when those neurochemical alarm bells ring, your brain presumes there's a good reason.

But if you give up on direct interpersonal trust, your brain feels that something is missing. Oxytocin is missing. You can wire yourself to trust without triggering your own alarm. Every time you feel good about an animal, or a large group, or an on-line relationship, tell yourself "I am creating this good feeling." It may sound silly or self-centered, but it builds confidence in your oxytocin pathway. If you focus on the trust in your life, you give it a chance to grow. Otherwise, your ability to distrust will keep growing.

Notice your trust feelings from any source for 45 days, and you will build a foundation that can support more.

Place stepping stones

Maybe there's someone you want to trust, but you can't bridge the divide in one leap. You can create intermediate steps that build trust gradually. The stepping stones can be placed so close together that neither party risks a big betrayal. Two people or two groups with an unfortunate history cannot always wipe the slate clean all at once. It's good to know you can build trust with a long series of very small interactions. The steps don't need to create complete trust, only positive expectations about the next step. Each small experience of trust stimulates the good feeling of oxytocin, and the neurons that can trigger it again.

Divorce lawyers use this strategy to help a couple reach agreement. You might try it with the person who is "ruining your life." Initiate a small interaction with someone who has disappointed you in the past. Though it's hard to trust someone who has betrayed you, you can arrange something tiny. If that proceeds without disaster, you may be comfortable doing it again. The goal is not to blindly trust and get disappointed. The goal is to build positive expectations.

This is hard work, and it won't feel good in the short run. But in the long run, it builds confidence that you can do something about the thorns in your side.

Coexisting without trust is draining. But it's even worse to take a leap of faith and get disappointed again by your crazy neighbor or the co-worker who stabbed you in the back. Where baseline trust is low due to a history of conflict, you can build up to a comfortable level in small increments.

You can't time it exactly since you are working with another person's responses. But you can decide to spend 45 days crafting reciprocal exchanges that build stepping stones toward trust with difficult people. Whether or not you succeed with any one particular person, you will build the good feeling of having some control over the trust bonds in your life. That feeling is an oxytocin circuit.

Be trustworthy

Oxytocin works both ways. When other people trust you, it feels good whether or not you trust them. You can create opportunities for other people to trust you.

Handle this strategy with care. You do not want to be the rescuer of everyone you know 45 days from now. Your goal is simply to feel the pleasure of another person's trust for a moment each day. Of course you can't force other people to trust you, and it may take more than a moment to extend yourself in ways that build trust. Do not spend a lot of time seeking approval. Simply honor your commitments, and then pause to enjoy being a person who honors their commitments. It may sound self-important, but the circuit it builds is the foundation of future trust. So plan to honor your commitments scrupulously for 45 days.

Count your change

You can practice the old adage, "trust, but verify." That may sound harsh, but verifying makes it possible to develop trust with strangers. If you're too nice to verify, you can get stuck inside the safe harbor of people you already trust.

To venture beyond, you have to interact with people whose trustworthiness is unknown. By trusting and verifying, new trust grows. If you do it for 45 days, you can't predict what others will do, but you can build confidence in your ability to extend your trust circle. Instead of being confined to the niche where you don't have to count your change, you have a tool for taking controlled risks.

Do not grow your circle by trusting people who are not trustworthy. The goal is not to trust as an end in itself, but to gather information about where you can trust. You succeed whether the other person shortchanges you or not, because you will have built a verification plan that works. Celebrate that each day, whether your trust is rewarded or disappointed.

Natural selection rewarded those who fanned out from familiar turf. In the animal world, young males are often ousted from their natal groups or leave on their own initiative because they're excluded from mating opportunities. According to blood samples taken in the wild, they experience huge stress when they leave those they trust for parts unknown. Their stress rises further when they seek admittance to a new troop, because the males of that troop reject potential rivals. But the seekers don't give up. Mammals keep seeking bonds of trust because it feels great when they succeed.

New oxytocin strategies	☺

© 2012 L. Breuning

Get a massage

Massage stimulates oxytocin. You don't have to spend a lot of money to have a daily massage. You can start a reciprocal exchange with a massage buddy, and build skill in a brief community-education class. Self-massage methods are surprisingly effective, too. The qi-gong self-massage technique requires no special strength and it's easy to learn from a video. Once you create the habit of stimulating your oxytocin in this way, it's a pleasure that will always be available to you.

Building New Serotonin Circuits

Take pride in what you've done

Developing pride is tricky. On the one hand, you know that seeking applause can have bad side effects. But when you get no recognition from others, something feels wrong. You could applaud yourself, but the brain is not easily tricked by hollow self-respect. It wants respect from others because that has survival value. There is no guaranteed, safe way to get this serotonin boost, alas. Social recognition is unpredictable and fleeting.

You can stimulate your serotonin without being "a jerk." Simply express pride in something you've done once a day. Pride is a rudder that helps you navigate opportunities to get social recognition. It helps you steer between the opposite extremes of constant approval-seeking and dejected cynicism.

Taking pride in yourself means more than silent meditation. It means daring to say "Look what I've done!" to another living soul. Asking others to respect your accomplishment is risky because you may be disappointed. People often protect themselves by insisting that social respect doesn't matter, or it's hopelessly unfair. But these rationales don't soothe the mammal brain's longing for the sense of security that social respect brings.

So every day for 45 days, you will say "Look what I've done" and expect a positive reaction. If you don't get the reaction you hope for, it will not kill you. The bad feeling will pass and the next day you will crow with a positive expectation again. If you already have negative expectations, this is hard to do. But if you force yourself to crow for five seconds a day for 45 days, you will find the social respect you expect.

You don't want to be a person who will do anything for attention. But many of the people we admire today got little respect while they were alive. They kept working without knowing the respect would come when they were not there to enjoy it.

Conversely, people who get lots of public applause often complain that they feel trapped by it. They say they'd rather do something different, but they fear losing the applause.

Whether you get a lot of social regard or a little, your brain will keep longing for it. That's what our mammal brain does. And that's why we need the skill of taking pride in our own accomplishments instead of waiting for applause.

If you focus on your shortcomings, you tend to overlook the applause you already have. More important, you may be getting quiet respect that is not expressed as audible applause. That's why it's useful to force yourself to expect appreciation for one moment a day. It allows you to take in what is already there.

Enjoy your position in each moment

When mammals gather, they try to dominate each other. If you always take the subordinate position to avoid conflict, you get frustrated. But if you always seek the dominant position, that has its frustrations too. Since both positions have pros and cons, and you can't have absolute control over which one you're in, why not just enjoy the pros instead of focusing on the cons?

Being in the subordinate position has a positive side. Someone else is in the "hot seat." You're not responsible for protecting others, and you don't have to worry about defending your position.

The positive side of the dominant position is the pleasure of getting respect, and the freedom to make choices instead of being subordinated to the will of others.

Your status will always be going up and down. If you fret over your position, the fretting will never end. Instead, you can enjoy the benefits of wherever you find yourself. For 45 days, notice your status frustrations and remind yourself of the hidden advantages of wherever you are. Once you make this a habit, you will want to do it always. Your mammal brain is always keeping track of your status, as much as you wish it wouldn't. This is a way to make peace with it.

Notice your influence

Many people look for the bad in others. They feel good about themselves in comparison, and that triggers serotonin. But this pleasure comes at a high price. You surround yourself with bad will. A slight change can give you the same serotonin boost without the side effects. Simply enjoy your influence on others. Without being arrogant or controlling or critical, you can make a habit of noticing when others mirror your good example. Don't expect credit or a thank you. Just feel good about it.

This may sound arrogant. But every brain longs to be important, and if you don't meet that need in healthy ways, you will be tempted to meet it in ways that have bad side effects. Everyone wants to have a impact on the world. No one wants to die without a trace. Some people even settle for having a bad impact, just to feel their own influence. There is an alternative.

You are already having an impact on the world. Right this minute, people may be respecting you behind your back. If your antennae are busy looking for disrespect, you won't know it. People may be secretly admiring you, and instead of enjoying it, you may be anticipating criticism from them. You're wasting the potential serotonin booster.

You can stop once a day to appreciate your good effect on others. Don't call attention to it or say "I told you so." Simply take quiet satisfaction in your subtle influence on the world. If you do this for 45 days, you will become alert to the ways in which you have influenced others. You will be less frustrated by their flaws and by their neglect. You will have a mental pathway for feeling your importance when you need to.

Parents often bemoan their lack of influence. If they knew how much their kids really are influenced by them in the long run, they would pay more attention to the example they set.

Make friends with something you can't control

Your brain feels good when you're in charge. It searches for things you can control, and avoids things you can't control. But much of the time our control is limited, so frustration percolates. You can learn to feel comfortable with your limited control instead. That doesn't mean giving up and living out of control. It means feeling safe while you're not in control.

You can build this circuit by giving up a habit that usually helps you feel "on top of things." For example, if you are a person who tries to bake the perfect souffle, spend 45 days cooking without recipes. But if you pride yourself on coloring outside the lines, courageously stay inside the lines for 45 day.

If you are a person who likes everything neat, trying having one space where you let junk pile up for six weeks. And if you are a person who hates order and loves chaos, be a neatnik for six weeks. It might feel awful on Day One, but you have 44 more days to try and fail and accept that.

Getting rid of the clock is a great way to experiment with control. No one can control time. We manage this harsh reality in different ways– constant lateness for some, and constant clock-checking for others. Here are some small ways to ignore the clock and make friends with the passage of time.

Try starting an activity without having an exact time you need to stop, and finish the activity without ever checking the clock the whole time. It's over when you feel like it's over.

Set aside a time each day during which you have no advance plan.

Designate a day in which you wake up without looking at the clock, and go about your business with no time-checking.

No matter how busy you are, you can find a way to stop submitting to the clock for a few minutes a day. You may be surprised at the bad feelings that come up, as much as you think you want to be free of time pressure. The bad feelings won't kill you, however, and accepting them helps you accept the fact that you can't control time.

The mammal brain feels good when it dominates, but you can't count on dominating all the time. That's why people like things that give them the feeling of being in charge. Some people love to break traffic laws, and others love to scold people who break traffic laws. Whatever you do to feel important, it can't work all the time. Some of the time you will feel unimportant. That triggers cortisol, but you can teach your brain that you are safe even when you feel unimportant.

Instead of trying to control the world in your accustomed ways, try giving up control for 45 days. Don't quit your job and beg with a rice bowl. Just stop checking the weather report. Stop buying lottery tickets. Stop expecting the world to work according to your rules. Choose one habit you have for feeling in control, and do without it. If you can't give up your control ritual completely, commit to giving it up for a certain time each day. You will end up feeling safe in the world despite your inability to control it.

New serotonin strategies	:)

© 2012 L. Breuning

Circuit-Training for Your Brain

Building new circuits is hard because it feels wrong when you're doing it right. Old circuits give you the feeling of knowing what's going on, so abandoning them for a weak and unproven circuit feels like a survival threat. Once the new circuit is established, you feel great. But that doesn't get to happen if you give up and rush back to the security of the old one. Here are some tools to help keep you blazing the new trail.

Mirror

Find people who already have the habit you'd like to create, and watch them. Your mirror neurons will light up and that will get your circuits going. This is a great way to overcome inertia because those initial connections are the hardest to spark.

Modeling people can be awkward, and the person with the habit you seek may not be aware of that habit in words. And that person may have other bad habits! Mirroring is a surgical tool. You don't substitute another person's judgement for your own. You just model their facility with a specific behavior that your own judgement aspires to. The world is full of people who have the behavior you need, and they'd love to show you how.

Balance

Your brain wants all four of the happy chemicals. You are probably better at some than others. It's tempting to choose projects in the areas you're already good at. But your brain will benefit more if you give it the happy chemical it has been missing. You may have to enter unknown territory to do that, but higher risk brings higher rewards.

If you are already a dopamine kind of person who's good at setting goals and meeting them, you might do more for yourself by working on a different happy chemical. If you're already an oxytocin kind of person, good at social bonding, you'd get higher returns by investing your effort in a different area. If you're a serotonin-focused person, good at winning respect, developing other happy-chemical circuits would help you flourish. And if you tend to be an endorphin person, drawn to mastering pain, you could benefit from focusing elsewhere.

When you depend on one happy chemical more than others, you don't know what's missing. You equate happiness with the kind you already know. So try a project from each of the four happy chemicals. Your brain will thank you.

Balancing your neurochemistry is not the same as "work-life balance." It's true that some people spend too much time working and neglect other ways of meeting their needs. But if you had more free time and spent it running the same circuits, you still wouldn't get neurochemical balance. If you manage your home the way you manage at work, then more time at home wouldn't make you happier. It would be like a vegetarian seeking balance with a new vegetable or an athlete seeking balance with a new sport. You keep seeking rewards in familiar places until you discover other places.

The good news is that a little bit of the neurochemical you lack goes a long way. You don't need to make big changes to feel big results. Your brain rewards you for taking the neural road-not-taken. But it won't release the new happy chemical immediately. It takes time to build the infrastructure.

Graft

You can graft a new branch onto the roots of a happy circuit you've already developed. I have often used my love of color to make difficult things fun. Every time I had to move, I looked forward to coloring my new home. When I work on my websites, I enjoy designing the colors. It seems trivial, but a trivial amount of spice makes all the difference in your enjoyment of a dish.

Grafting can help balance your neurochemicals. An activity that triggers one happy chemical can be grafted in a way that triggers the others. Let's say you love photography. It triggers dopamine when you seek and find a particular shot. It can stimulate oxytocin if you share the images with others. And serotonin flows if you enter your pictures in exhibitions. You can stimulate what you're missing within the activity you love.

Let's say you're a person who loves parties. You're already good at stimulating oxytocin in this way, and if you plan parties you can stimulate dopamine. You might work on fund-raisers or political events to stimulate serotonin. New happy chemicals are easier to spark when you build onto existing roots.

Many people connect to old flames in later life. This clearly grafts new good feelings onto old roots. Another common grafting strategy is returning to a hobby you loved as a child. Building a hobby into a career is another. New happy circuits are hard to build, so adding branches to an existing tree can help.

When I retired from academia, I began judging science fairs. I love this new limb on my old trunk. I meet kids that I deeply respect, and they are thrilled to have professional attention to their work.

Legacy

Anything connected to your DNA triggers happy chemicals. Traditionally, people doted on grandchildren as they aged, which created a tangible sense of their legacy. Many alternative ways to feel good about your legacy are popular today. Whether you research your ancestry or preserve your family traditions, it makes your brain feel good. You don't consciously connect it to your genes, but it builds on a connection that's already there. Even if you just buy pizza for a niece or nephew, you feed your mammal brain's interest in the survival of your genes. You can say genes don't matter, but your brain has a curious way of perking up at anything involving your genes.

Connecting with children rewards the urge for legacy, even if they're not your own. If you do have your own children, every moment with them is part of your legacy whether it's obvious in the moment or not. I figured this out when my son's school closed for teacher training. I heard parents complaining about the inconvenience of all the extra no-school days, and I had that "I should be working" feeling too. Then I learned to see it as a gift. An excuse to take a day off and do something meaningful with my kids was being handed to me. I would be crazy to see it as a burden.

You can define your legacy however you want. You can reorganize the equipment at your gym. You can invent a new stitch that lives on at your knitting club. It doesn't have to make logical sense. When you see that something of yourself will live on, it's strangely effective in triggering your happy chemicals.

Fun

New circuits grow easily when repetition is fun. I had fun learning foreign languages by traveling and watching foreign films. Many people learn English by watching TV, and humans have always excelled at learning languages "on the pillow," as they say in French (*sur l'oreiller*).

Building a new circuit requires more repetition than most people can tolerate. If you don't find a way to make it fun, you may not keep at it. One reason adults don't build new neural circuits is that they neglect the power of fun. You have to find new kinds of fun if you want to build new circuits, or you'll be stuck in the pathways of old amusements. Of course, you shouldn't limit yourself to things that are fun. But if you can find the fun in a task you need to master, it helps you persist long enough to pave the circuit.

Chunk

The brain can only process a few inputs at a time, so it divides new things into chunks. We are always making sense of the world by organizing the chaos of raw detail into manageable chunks. Dividing up challenges makes them easier to tackle. One of my students told me he bicycles to the top of a mountain by dividing it into quarters, and celebrating each intermediate goal. Logically that makes no sense since the mountain is still just as high. But chunking succeeds at tricking your brain into feeling good even when you're not really fooled.

I tried it on my own "mountain"– the mess in my garage. I was amazed at how well it worked. My husband and I both dreaded the chore, but longed to have it done. I suggested that we do it for fifteen minutes, and leave the rest for another day. I thought we would get it done in fifteen-minute chunks. But once we got started, we didn't feel like stopping. When we stood at the bottom of the junk mountain and looked up, we couldn't get ourselves to start. But when we set our sights on an easy goal, we expected to succeed. The good feeling it triggered led to success, more positive expectations, and more good feelings. Small sparks lit a fire of enthusiasm.

Favorite circuit-builders	:)

Patience

It takes time for electricity to zip through new pathways. Forty-five days may seem like a long time to repeat something. If you're tempted to stop in less than forty-five days, think of it as prescription medicine that you have to finish even if your symptoms are gone. New happy strategies won't feel effortful forever. After a few weeks, they'll just feel good, and they'll stay with your forever.

Accept

I can always think of ways I could have done better, even when I do well. If I succeed at building a new circuit, I wonder why I didn't do it a long time ago. When I see an adorable toddler, I wonder why I don't remember more of my children's toddlerhood. Then I realize I am creating unnecessary disappointment. Struggling to optimize constantly can lead to frustration. Life is precious and we naturally want to make the most of it. But optimization may not trigger happy chemicals. Sometimes, you get more by accepting what is. When I find it hard to stop optimizing, I remind myself that the 1978 Nobel Prize in Economics was awarded for a mathematical proof that "satisficing" is better than optimizing.

Plan

Build a new circuit before you need it. Expose yourself to new music before your current faves bore you, and make new friends before you need them. Before you retire and get wrinkles, develop new sources of pride. You may feel too busy to do these things. But once they trigger happy chemicals, you'll be glad you did. Instead of waiting for happy chemicals to come your way, plan to "do something."

Planning can relieve unhappy chemicals, too. You can plan to worry while brushing your teeth, and relinquish anxiety the rest of the day. If that's not enough worry time, plan to do it while you're flossing as well. In 45 days, you may love the results.

You can re-wire yourself if you're willing to go about it systematically. You can find peace without the habits that are currently causing distress. With so many strategies to choose from, why would anyone reject them all and effectively choose to be unhappy instead? The following chapter shows that people choose unhappiness for reasons that are so familiar we take them for granted.

6
Choosing Unhappiness

If you could be happy in 45 days with just a few minutes of effort per day, why wouldn't you? Here are common rationales for sticking with unhappy thought habits instead of substituting happier ones. Each has its own vicious cycle.

Reason #1: "I can't lower my standards"

I have high aspirations, you may think. Why should I be happy with small things?

It's natural to assume big things will make you happy, since we've all felt big spurts from big achievements. But big achievers are not necessarily happy people. This is hard to believe, but tabloid news does a public service by reminding us.

In modern times, people with "high standards" often focus on "saving the world." They say it's unethical to be happy as long as one person in the world is suffering, or even one animal. But the world has always been full of suffering. Is it unethical for anyone in human history to have ever been happy? No. Your cortex might embrace "ethics" as an explanation for the unhappiness your mammal brain is producing. A cortex constructs verbal logic for neurochemicals that can't speak.

Perhaps you think happiness is just handed to some people, while others are wrongly deprived of it. Perhaps you think suffering is the way to earn happiness. Such thoughts create a vicious cycle. You feel good for a moment when you ally yourself with suffering and deprivation. You feel important and bonded, so serotonin and oxytocin flow. But the good feelings soon stop, and you try to get more by suffering more, because that's the link you've built.

There is an alternative. You can accept that everyone has to manage their own brain. Every brain is always releasing happy and unhappy chemicals using the circuits it has. You decide how to manage your brain. No one else is responsible for your brain, and you are not responsible for other people's brains.

If you take an idealized view of happiness, it will always be out of reach. You might blame others for this. You might think permanent happiness would reign if it weren't for the bad guys who lack your "high standards." You might focus on saving the world from those bad guys to somehow "get" the happiness they've deprived you of.

While you are waiting for the world to meet your high standards, you might engage in bad habits to relieve your frustration. You justify these happy habits by pointing to the flaws of the world. This vicious circle is a common by-product of "high standards." You'd be better off learning to be happy with small things than waiting for the world to be perfect.

Well-intentioned people choose unhappiness without realizing it. Teachers often choose unhappiness for their students by insisting on impossible standards. Imagine a teacher encouraging all his students to aspire to be president. He's condemning them to disillusion and frustration when they fall short. And even presidents experience unhappiness and must learn to manage it. When teachers require literacy and math skills, students learn the self-management habits that lead to happiness in the real world.

"High standards" sound nice, but it can be an excuse for living with bitterness and resentment while you're waiting for some abstract ideal. Your high standards can lead to low standards if you exclude a realistic middle ground. Meeting your own survival needs is the standard your brain evolved for, so that is what makes you feel good.

Reason #2: "I shouldn't have to do this"

You may be thinking, "Other people get to be happy without repeating things for 45 days. Why should I have to?"

Maybe you think other people owe you something, so why should you "let the jerks off the hook" by making yourself happy. You expect "the jerks" to make you happy when they give you what you think you deserve.

Maybe you think you've done more than enough, and it's time for the rest of the world to do its part.

Many people think settling a score with those who have short-changed them is the path to happiness. Once you look at life this way, you will easily find evidence that you have been wronged and lots of company to share your view.

I've often heard students say it's unfair they have to work hard at coursework while someone they know seems to "get it" effortlessly. I often hear dieters say it's unfair that others stay thin effortlessly.

If you think happiness comes effortlessly to others, you might decide that it's unfair for you to have to work at it.

When you feel wronged by life, you give yourself permission to have another cookie, or another drink, or another pill, or another sulk. After all you've been through, why deprive yourself anymore? This is a vicious cycle. You keep feeling wronged in order to enjoy more of your consolation prize.

It's easy to believe others are luckier than you in the happy-circuit department. We mammals naturally compare ourselves to others. But we never really know the inside story about other people's lives. Even if you could know, it wouldn't make you happy. Focusing on other people's emotional accounting diverts you from doing what it takes to trigger your own happy chemicals.

If you are always searching for wrongs, you don't notice what's right, even if you stumble on it. And yet, this mindset is curiously popular. You wire it in when you are young, pleasing teachers with essays on the awful state of the world, and mirroring parents who feel deprived themselves.

Some people have no experience making themselves happy because they grew up in a world in which other people took responsibility for their happiness. Some parents live to please their children and never please themselves. Their children learn to expect others to please them, and they don't learn to please themselves either. When they're unhappy, they are sure someone else messed up.

Blaming others for your unhappiness is a habit that's hard to give up because it triggers some happy chemicals. You feel important when you battle perceived injustice (serotonin), and you bond with others who feel similarly deprived (oxytocin). You get excited when you seek and find evidence that you have been denied your fair share of happiness (dopamine). You may even trigger endorphin by welcoming physical pain into your life as evidence of your deprivation. You keep building a circuit for seeking happiness by feeling wronged.

A stopped clock is right twice a day, so if you look for evidence that happiness is wrongfully distributed to the undeserving, you will certainly find it. But it will only make you happy for a moment. Then you will need to go find more evidence that "they" have failed to distribute happiness in equal shares. You will not learn to produce happiness yourself while distracted by the belief that happiness is doled out by "them."

You can be happy by building new circuits. Six weeks from now, you might be the happiest person you know. But you won't do what it takes if you believe you shouldn't have to. If you focus on the happiness you think others are "getting," you end up shortchanging yourself.

Reason #3: "It's selfish to focus on your own happiness"

Many people take a zero-sum view of happiness. They unconsciously believe that one person's happiness takes away from others. When my mother was scrubbing the floor in an angry rage, she felt sure that she would be happy if only I were scrubbing the floor instead of her. So I got down and scrubbed, preferring that to being labelled "selfish." But it failed to make my mother happy. I felt like the captain who had to go down with the sinking ship. But I learned that I was not captain of her ship. I could only be captain of my own.

Looking back, I understand that my mother wanted company. She didn't know how to stop scrubbing, so she wanted me to join her in her prison. "Our society" was not forcing her to scrub. It's a habit she built long ago, when it seemed to promote survival. She navigated her survival choices, and I navigated mine.

Learning to stimulate my own happy chemicals does not deprive others of them. Each adult is free to make their own calls in the pursuit of happiness as long as they take responsibility for their own side effects. Adults must not make themselves happy at the expense of children. But when you are with other adults, you are not obligated to subordinate your happiness to theirs. Cooperating in pursuit of mutual goals is a great way to promote survival. And trust enables us to do that without one-for-one reciprocity. But if someone insists you must subordinate your survival needs to theirs, you don't have to agree.

If you give yourself permission to feel good while others are feeling bad, you are helping them more than you realize. Other people's mirror neurons will notice and spark happiness, too. But you cannot make yourself happy for the purpose of helping others. That's a contradiction in terms. Your brain rewards you for promoting your survival, not for denying your needs. If you decide to be happy, you may feel conspicuous and out of step with those who decide differently. You may be tempted to feign suffering to avoid being called "selfish." You get to choose, and live with the consequences.

Perhaps you enjoy the feeling of unselfishly devoting your life to others. The thought of "changing the world" triggers your happy chemicals. You may think you only care about the planet and the underprivileged, but your brain is focused on you. Your world-changing efforts trigger serotonin because they get respect and build a legacy. Oxytocin flows as you join forces with fellow world-changers. Dopamine surges when you set goals and accomplish them. You are focusing on your own happiness. Being a rescuer is so rewarding that many rescuers persist when they do more harm than good. They ignore the harmful consequences of their intercession because they don't know how else to get those selfish rewards.

Adulthood means creating a sense of well-being that's separate from others. *Enmeshment* is what psychologists call it when a person can't distinguish their own neurochemistry from others.' Enmeshment lures people with the immediate reward you get from taking charge of other people's happiness, or from the expectation that others will take charge of yours. The result is often shared suffering.

The problem is that you have to keep suffering to keep getting the reward. If you are afraid to be caught looking happy while others are suffering, you will always find suffering to join in with. Many people focus on the suffering of the planet, or animals, or far-away children. It's a way to avoid looking "selfish" while still putting a little distance between yourself and the suffering.

It's reasonable to feel bad about the suffering of others, and it's reasonable to help where you can. But being a good person does not mean enmeshment. When you stay focused on your own brain, you are not judging or abandoning others. You are unselfishly respecting their responsibility for their own brain. You are securing your own oxygen mask. If you put your happiness in other people's hands instead, you're likely to end up in a vicious cycle.

People may sneer at you if you don't join in the suffering. In the past, people were tortured and executed if they refused to join the shared belief system. So when people sneer at me for not joining in an unhappy thought habit, I'm just grateful that sneering is such a small penalty.

Reason #4: "I want to be ready when it hits the fan"

Will you lose your edge if you let yourself be happy? Will it lower your guard, leaving you worse off when things go wrong?

If you believe this, you make it true. Your brain can always find potential threats, and if you focus on them, that is the world your brain will know. You will not see the good in the world unless you are looking for it because the cortex finds the information it looks for. Your brain is always choosing which details to focus on because it's impossible to process everything. It has to choose quickly in order to function, so it scans for patterns that match its expectations.

If you look for the good in life, you may feel like you're frittering your attention and taking your eye off the ball. But ironically, focusing on potential crises does not necessarily prepare you for them. Bad things are curiously unpredictable. A siege mentality just wears you out. Happiness builds a cushion that prepares you for bumpy roads better than unhappiness.

Happiness is less distracting than you may think. It's the side effects that cause people to presume happiness conflicts with survival. You can build happy circuits that have fewer side effects.

While you're building new circuits, you may have a bad feeling that stuff is hitting the fan. That's your old superhighways lighting up. If you keep focusing on good things for 45 days instead of giving all your attention to those crisis-mentality circuits, you will have a new superhighway. You will see more in the world than potential calamity.

If you choose instead to focus on disaster preparedness, you're in a vicious cycle. Every time your happy chemicals dip, you expect a cataclysm and start preparing. That keeps you focused on danger signals, which triggers more unhappy chemicals, which motivates more preparedness.

You can end this vicious cycle in one instant, just by refusing to give your attention to a threat when it pops into your mind. It may feel bad. You may feel like you will die if you don't do something about the looming crisis. But you will survive that instant, and you will courageously refuse to contemplate disaster for the next instant, too. Eventually, you will create a gap big enough to fill with positive expectations. A happy circuit will grow big enough to compete for your attention.

And when things go wrong, you can ask yourself whether being unhappy would have prevented it.

Reason #5: "I won't be able to do this"

What if you try to build new circuits and fail? The thought sounds so bad that your old circuits seem comparatively happy.

If you expect to fail, 45 days is a very long time. You'd rather not try than spend 45 days worried about blowing it.

Failure is easy to imagine because that's where your existing pathways lead. If your existing circuits could imagine a new habit, you'd already be doing it. So the challenge is to start without a clear conception of the finish.

If you expect to do things right the first time, disappointment is likely. If you refuse to do things until you're sure of doing them right, you limit yourself significantly. Willingness to fail gives you power. It frees you from doing the same old thing over and over. Tolerance for failure doesn't mean expecting to fail. It means expecting to succeed after a period of trial and error. The error is not a sign of incompetence; it's a sign that you are facing up to an unknown that must be explored before it can be mastered.

But each time we fail, it triggers memory of past failures. No one likes being reminded of past failures. If Day One of your circuit building unleashes the spirit of everything you've ever done wrong, it's hard to continue on Day Two.

But if you give up on Day Two, your failure circuit is strengthened. It's a vicious cycle that only you can stop by doing something that feels temporarily bad. Tell yourself "I did it!," even if the only thing you did was thinking "I did it!" while feeling like you can't do it.

It will probably feel fake at first. But if you persist, the success feeling will become a circuit that's big enough to feel as true as the failure circuit.

Of course, you don't want to be a deluded person who pats himself on the back for no reason. But you may already be kicking yourself for no reason. Accidents of experience will define you until you shape new experiences into new circuits.

Building a success circuit doesn't mean lying to yourself and others. It means you can be honest about failure because you "know" that trial and error leads to success.

Reason #6: "Who can be happy in such a flawed society?"

My college professors taught me to blame "the system" for all human misery. They praised anything that linked human problems to the flaws of "our society." And they disdained anyone who questioned this view, saying "they don't get it." I didn't want to be dismissed as stupid or evil, so I "got it".

I eventually understood the flaws in their reasoning. I learned that tearing down the system leads to more unhappiness. I learned that people who have things given to them are as unhappy as people who are considered "deprived." I learned that human nature is more complicated than the lyrics to a 1960s folk song would suggest. Happy chemicals only come in brief spurts. We cannot be on an emotional high every moment. If we blame the system for that, it feels good for a moment, but it's a vicious cycle. Blaming boosts your self-respect, but you have to feel hopeless about the world to get that boost.

Blaming abstract institutions protects you from blaming people you know in person. That keeps the peace with friends and family in the short run, but you don't work things out with flesh-and-blood people when your attention is focused on an abstract "them."

Each time your happy chemicals dip, you might soothe yourself with visions of the world being "fixed" in a way that will make you happy all the time. Instead of building healthy new ways to stimulate your happy chemicals, you might imagine you live in a hell because the system is flawed and the bad guys block change.

This thought habit surrounded me for decades. Wherever I went, I heard the expression "our society is bad." I had a large circuit to welcome this input. But the more I studied history, the more I understood the miseries of the past. I realized that our lives are good, and I was stunned at how few people notice. In fact, people seemed indignant if I mentioned any positives. It seems like the rallying cries of starving serfs in France and Russia are copied and pasted into today's discussions without anyone noticing the unprecedented improvement in their quality of life. A new generation has grown up being told that they are living in misery under an oppressive system. They get "A"s if they reproduce this view, and they're ostracized if they challenge it. They don't want to be condemned as stupid or evil, so they "get it."

Many people believe they cannot change unless everyone else changes. They can't stop eating junk food until "our society stops eating junk food." They can't stop feeling shame until "our society stops shaming you." They can't stop worrying about their future until "our society takes care of the future." If you put our society in charge of your brain, you are in a terrible bind. When you put yourself in charge of your own happiness, you will do what it takes.

"The personal is political" was a popular slogan when I was young. Early feminists promoted the idea that problems in your personal life are caused by political failures and must be solved by political action. This prescription triggers good feelings in the short run. But those who expect the government to solve their personal problems end up disappointed. Human relations are difficult, and if political anger is your primary tool for working through these difficulties, you are likely to get bad results.

I have learned to see the reverse: "the political is personal." Our personal frustrations get projected onto the political system. When unhappy chemicals get your attention, blaming the political system is one way to feel good again. But to feel good you have to keep believing your society is bad and your life is bad. Politics diverts you from making peace with the uncomfortable facts of life. You are just one person among seven billion. Some day you will die, and the world will spin on without you. It's not the government's fault, and blaming the government for the awful truth can distract you from making the most of the time you have.

Your brain is designed to see you as the center of the world. But when you go out and interact with people, you are constantly reminded that you are not the center of the world. This is so unpleasant that your brain cries out "Something must be done about it!" You can join with others who feel the same way, and "demand that your voice be heard." But when you expect public institutions to satisfy that deep human longing to be heard, you get disappointed. You try again. It's a vicious cycle that distracts you from the real people in your life that don't hear you either. Each brain gets frustrated about being heard because we built circuits in youth, when being ignored truly was a full survival emergency.

Everyone has to manage this core unhappiness. If those around you manage it by hating people in suits, it's easy to do that, too. But you end up full of hate. Instead of blaming society for the frustrations of being a mammal, you can learn to accept the mammalian facts of life. You will feel less frustrated if you do.

But questioning the system-failure theory of human happiness can damage careers and relationships that you've nurtured for years. If you succeed at changing yourself, you may get a bad reaction from people who still believe they cannot be happy until the world changes. They may label you "privileged," and start blaming their unhappiness on you. But you didn't create the mammal brain.

We have no choice but to live in a world where everyone else has a mammal brain focused on its own survival. Those who refuse to see their own mammalian nature may get angry about the mammalian nature of others. But we are fortunate to live in an age where our nature is increasingly well understood.

Accepting responsibility for your own happiness can be anxiety-provoking at first. The urge to "do something" never seems to stop. You might prefer the relative calm of just waiting for a "revolution" to bring a "good society." When you stop believing the system can make you happy, you are stuck with the awful prospect of doing it yourself. It's much easier to tussle with philosophical abstractions than to deal with actual people who get on your nerves. It's easier to think about fixing the system than to think about fixing yourself.

Believing in a system that makes everyone happy is comforting. It may be the only path to happiness for those who decide it's wrong to make yourself happy. Imagining this "better world" feels so good that it can become your primary happy circuit. But while you wait for the better world in the long run, you overlook your own power to make your life better in the short run.

Changing yourself is hard, while "changing the world" seems like fun. When you get frustrated trying to change yourself, it seems easier to get frustrated with "the system." Raging at the system creates social bonds, a feeling of social dominance, and the expectation of future rewards. It stimulates happy chemicals fast. Changing yourself does not feel good unless you keep at it for a while. It's not surprising that so many people focus on changing others instead of themselves.

Reason #7: "I'll be happy when..."

People often imagine they will be happy when they reach some particular benchmark in their public or private life. We imagine happiness will come as a result of "making it" in some area or another. I'll be happy when I can finish a triathlon, or get my grandchildren into a good pre-school, or stop AIDS.

But goals are double-edged swords. They stimulate happy chemicals because you link them to survival. But they also stimulate unhappy chemicals because your brain sees every obstacle to your goal as a survival threat. Of course, you know you can survive without winning the Olympics in Stand-up Comedy, but your cortisol tells you otherwise.

Goals do stimulate happy chemicals. Dopamine surges when you approach rewards, and serotonin flows when you take pride in your accomplishment. Oxytocin is boosted when you bond with others in pursuit of your goal, and even endorphin is triggered if you push yourself to the point of pain. But goals cause a vicious cycle if you use them to mask unhappy chemicals. You constantly focus on a goal because you can't stand it when your happy chemicals dip, and you end up feeling exhausted and resentful. You think you can't stop until you "get a break" and reach that milestone you imagine. Once you "get it right," you quickly focus on a new goal and start feeling overwhelmed again.

Reasons I choose unhappiness	

You can't stop this loop if it's the only one you have. Single-minded pursuit of a goal can lead you to see other people as obstacles. You might see your body as an obstacle. You might even see rules and laws as obstacles. If you imagine yourself on an escalator to perfection, unhappy chemicals stun you when you step off the escalator.

People often say "our society" forces this on them. They don't see how they've created this loop, though they can easily see that in others. The urge to "make something of yourself" is much older than our society. Status feels good, and the urge for status has motivated people to do useful things. But the mammalian brain keeps seeking more status to keep feeling good. You may dream of a world in which your status anxiety is gone. But you will always live in the world of your mammal brain. All you can do is create new pathways to your happy chemicals.

You can free yourself from an escalator if you are willing to do something different for 45 days. Do not simply replace one goal with another. Instead, build the habit of having multiple sources of satisfaction. Your new circuits will not trigger happy chemicals every minute. But they help you survive that blast of unhappy chemical you feel when you ease off your goal.

Watching the news tends to reinforce the escalator view of happiness because it focuses on people with high social dominance. Your mirror neurons feel their confidence, and your mammal brain feels like you've been included in elite circles. Then your cortex realizes that you're not included. You have to make peace with your mammalian status urge. If you hate that urge, you hate yourself and everyone else. Instead, you can just accept it and decide where to invest your life energy.

We all invest effort with no guarantees of the outcome. You can never be sure when your efforts will be rewarded. But reaching goals doesn't ensure constant happiness, so you might as well start being happy before those goals are reached.

Choosing Happiness

Some thought patterns stimulate happy chemicals in the short run, but they lock you into unhappiness in the long run. You get to decide which thought habits are good for you. You are the master of the cockamamie mental equipment built by your life experience. The moment you refuse to send your electricity down an unhappy highway, you create space for a new thought pattern to grow. You can grow the happy habit you choose.

7
The Burden of Choice

The Trail of Trade-offs

There is no set path to happy chemicals. There is only a constant string of trade-offs. The choices are so hard to make that you might be tempted to shift the burden of choice onto others. When you let others choose for you, you may not like the results, but at least you can get angry with them instead of being angry with yourself.

Choice leads to cortisol when you fail to get what you seek. You might also end up with bad feelings if you get what you seek and start thinking about what it cost you. Trade-offs are inevitable because life is finite.

People are always deciding when to risk something to gain something else. We hear a lot about "good decisions" and "bad decisions," but every decision is bad when you look for the bad in it. Even when you're rewarded, you may focus on how you might have done slightly better. When you have two good choices in front of you, you might endlessly lament the option you didn't choose.

Frustration grows if you think of life as an optimization function with one correct solution. Instead, you can think of life as a series of trade-offs. Tough calls are inevitable, but you are the best judge of the fine-tuned trade-offs of your own life.

Your brain will never stop trying to promote your survival. It will take what you have for granted and look for ways to get more– more rewards (dopamine), more physical security (endorphin), more social support (oxytocin), more respect (serotonin). Seeking more is risky. Your brain is constantly deciding whether it's worth giving up some of this to get more of that. Once you decide, you may not get the outcome you expected. The resulting frustration may tempt you to leave the hard calls to someone else.

You will end up with more happy chemicals if you carry your own burden of choice. You can manage the frustration by accepting that trade-offs are inevitable in the real world. Here are some examples.

Short run vs. Long run

We constantly weigh immediate rewards against rewards we expect in the future. If you decide to smoke, you put a particular value on your present as opposed to your future. If you decide to party, you trade off a future reward for a present reward. You get to live with the consequences, which motivates you to make the best possible predictions about your well-being. Perfect predictions are impossible, but better information leads to better choices.

You are always choosing which information you focus on. You can choose good information and make good choices. You will not do that if you believe you are a victim of outside forces. When you know that your life depends on your choices, you get the information you need to manage your trade-offs.

Known vs. Unknown

We are always trading off the security of the known against the promise of the unknown. You can choose to stick with the known until you find an alternative that feels like a sure thing. Or you can risk an alternative before it's fully baked. Once you choose, you never know how the other option would have turned out.

However things go, you can make yourself feel worse by looking for flaws in your decision-making. Or you can make yourself feel better by honoring your ability to make choices amidst the inevitable uncertainty of life. I am not saying you should defend your decisions to the point of refusing to learn from experience. But if you only attack your decisions, you will never make a choice unless there's absolute certainty. Most of the time, uncertainty prevails. The better you can live with it, the more options you have.

Individual vs. Group

Going along with the group triggers one good feeling, and striking out on your own you triggers another. It would be nice to have both, but it's not realistic to expect that. When you're with the group, you might notice what you're missing and long for the good feeling of independent action. But when you follow your individual impulses, the loss of group protection feels bad to your mammal brain. There is no permanent solution, only constant trade-offs. When you go with the group, you will feel the squeeze on your personal interests. When you focus on yourself, you will feel the pressure on your social ties.

At some point you have to accept the conundrum. Though careful decisions are nice, you will have nothing but unhappy chemicals if you focus on the down side of each option. Instead, you could focus on the benefits of the option you are currently enjoying. Enjoy the group when it's group time and enjoy your individuality when you're alone. Your mind naturally seeks what it doesn't have, but you can remind it of what it has.

It's natural to want it all. You'd like to have more group support without losing your individuality. You'd like to focus more on your own needs without losing the support of the group. Why shouldn't I have it all, people think. Perhaps small adjustments are possible, but it's important to see that this trade off is part of being human. Instead of expecting it to go away, you can pride yourself on your ability to manage it.

Free will vs. Dependency

If you were a zoo animal, you might envy wild animals and try to break free. But if you were a wild animal, burdened by the need to root for food, compete for mates, and protect your offspring from predators, you might look for a way to break into the zoo for food and shelter.

Having your needs met by others looks nice, but people often end up disappointed with what they're getting and angry at the loss of freedom.

When you're free to meet your own needs, you might groan from the burden instead of celebrating it. Both paths have ups and downs, and the mind easily sees the down side because it wants to make things better. You can see the up side if you make a habit of looking for it.

Choice can be so frustrating that people sometimes opt to live in the zoo and then hate the zookeeper. People may want to be led and protected, but at the same time resent those with power over them. They often resolve this with perpetual hostility toward their leaders and providers. They create a sense of personal power by putting down those they perceive as above them. But it never really makes up for the sense of personal power they lose when they give away their burden of choice instead of managing it themselves.

Trade-offs I manage	😊

© 2012 L. Breuning

How You Keep Score

A lizard has simple decision rules. When he sees something bigger than himself, he runs from it. When he sees something smaller, he tries to eat it. And if it's about his size, he tries to mate with it. Then he moves on to the next thing.

A lizard doesn't analyze his successes and failures. He has neurochemical ups and downs, but he doesn't expect himself to produce ups all the time. You are able to judge yourself because you have enough neurons to compare yourself to abstract expectations. This helps you find ways to improve things in the future. The ability to judge yourself is a blessing unless you make it a curse.

A mouse fails to get the cheese some of the time. He tries again, but he doesn't kick himself for being an idiot. He has a much worse problem: hunger. You manage to avoid hunger because you anticipate your needs, and judge yourself when you fall short of meeting those needs. You expect to get the cheese every time, and if you choose the wrong path you feel bad, even when you have enough cheese.

Humans are always keeping score on themselves. Our cortex evolved to learn from experience. We often succeed at avoiding harm by learning from our failures. We can get so good at this that we overlook things that go right. We don't want to clutter our minds with information unless we can see how it helps us score.

Each person tries to improve their own "score" by learning from their own experience. When you score in your own mind, it feels great, briefly, and the happy chemicals wire you to score in that way in the future. When you fail to score, it hurts, and unhappy chemicals build a pathway that tells you how to avoid that kind of hurt in the future. You develop neural networks good at fixing problems so you can feel good. Your circuits can overlook good things around you because they don't seem relevant to your score.

You can train yourself to see what goes right instead of just seeing what goes wrong. It may feel dangerous because you are less focused on threats while you're scanning for triumphs. But if you tolerate that anxiety for a short time, your mammal brain gets the message that you will not die if you stop scanning for predators. At first, it will be hard to see triumphs because you haven't built neural superhighways for them to light up. But the pathways build if you keep at it.

I started thinking about what goes right when I came home from a year in Africa. Every time I flushed a toilet, I marveled that such a luxury exists. I realized that people lived without proper sewage systems for most of human history, and yet when we have them, we take them for granted. Rat-infested outhouses and open drainage ditches would make us very unhappy. Yet when sewage is whisked away from us effortlessly, it doesn't make us the slightest bit happy.

When I lived in Central African Republic, I got stuck in an elevator during one of the many blackouts. After that, I made a concerted effort to celebrate elevators instead of being scared of them. Every time an elevator works, I appreciate it instead of taking it for granted.

My appreciation of infrastructure began in Haiti, when I was invited to a picnic at a dam. Why would you want to picnic at a dam, I asked. I had lived in the world where dams were sneered at as blots on the landscape. My co-worker explained that electricity and drinking water were scarce, and the dam was widely seen as something to celebrate. Since then, every time I use water, I think about all it took to get it to me. When I wash a teacup, I imagine the quantity of water I've used in relation to the containers Haitian women carry on their heads. Instead of focusing on what goes wrong, I focus on what goes right.

During my stays in China, I went for lots of massages. Each one felt unique, and I marveled at the massage therapists' skill. More important, I marveled at the fact that I could walk into a public place and take my clothes off in perfect safety. That level of trust is a colossal achievement. In most of human history, it was not safe to leave your village. Strangers could easily kill you with impunity, and people rarely left their familiar hamlets in a lifetime. Now, strangers literally rub shoulders worldwide in safety. Things go wrong occasionally, but when you focus on problems you miss the immensity of what goes right.

When I lived abroad, I often saw food contaminated by insects, vermin, and grains of sand, not to mention invisible contaminants. People lived with contaminated food for most of human history, and they were grateful they weren't starving. Now, our food supply is virtually free of immediate threats, and most long-run threats too. No one I know seems to appreciate this. People seem to be in a frenzy about food risks with no idea of what has gone right.

When I get health care, I appreciate what goes right. I had a severe pneumonia in my thirties, and would probably not be alive today if it weren't for the antibiotics. They were introduced less than a decade before I was born. Most of us alive today would already have been done in by something if we hadn't had modern health care. Yet people rage at health care all the time with scarcely a thought of what goes right.

On the contrary, people often pride themselves on their expertise in what goes wrong. They end up in a vicious cycle, needing to focus on signs of disaster in order to keep feeling good about themselves.

Life is Like a Box of Chocolates

A box of chocolate confronts you with choice. Sometimes, your pick disappoints. Even worse, you may see someone else get the chocolate you'd hoped for. When a chocolate falls short of your expectations, it's possible to feel bad even while you're enjoying intense chocolatey goodness that's overwhelmingly similar to the other chocolates.

We all build expectations about what will make us happy. We feel good or bad by comparing our reality to what we expected. Our expectations build in adolescence because that's when the brain is highly plastic. These expectations are inevitably unrealistic. A young person imagines they'll feel on top of the world as soon as they can come and go without anyone telling them when to go to bed or take a test. But once you start meeting your own needs instead of having others meet your needs for you, you don't feel like you're master of the universe. You wonder what went wrong. Something is wrong with the world, you may think, or with your partner, your boss, your culture, yourself. You never blame the brain circuits that compare reality to your youthful enthusiasm, because those circuits function without your awareness.

I have a friend who always complains about the food he gets in a restaurant. He chose it himself, of course, but once it comes, it seems flawed to him. He looks longingly at other people's orders. When I eat with him, I feel like I can't enjoy my meal. So I no longer eat with this person.

You are always choosing the information you feed to your brain. Choice is a responsibility we can celebrate or dread. I often hear students complain that it's so hard to choose courses. But I also hear them complain when a course is required. When they don't have choice they lament it, but when they have it they don't seem to value it.

If you had lived in times past, you would have not been free to choose your career, your beliefs, or even your sex partner. Group expectations would have constrained you. You would have imagined eternal bliss if only you could choose your mate, your work, and the expletives you hurl at the powers that be. Yet these choices do not bring constant happiness when you have them. Your brain keeps looking for more and focusing on the obstacles.

When life is frustrating, people often blame "bad choices." This implies that there were clear "good choices" just hanging around that a person overlooked. Reality is more complicated. Each choice has its advantages and disadvantages. Once you embrace one choice, you see its disadvantages up close. If you had to do it over, you might make another "bad choice," because the down side of each option is hard to know until you've chosen. You can spend your whole life lamenting your choices, or accept the fleeting nature of happiness. Instead of focusing on what you would've-could've-should've had, you can see the good in what you've chosen. Even a "good choice" will only make you happy for a short time.

Your mammal brain evolved to work without conscious awareness. But modern science lets us choose to understand the neurochemical ups and downs our mammal brain produces in its wordless way. If you decide to be happy, your brain will find things to be happy about. You will still have frustrations and disappointments, but you will always have the ability to find ways to make yourself happy. If your happy pathways don't spark themselves, you will find healthy ways to crank them up.

You can do this right now. No one is stopping you. And you cannot do it for someone else.

Your happy chemicals cannot surge constantly. But you do not need to be having a "peak" experience all the time. When happy chemicals dip, unhappy chemicals may get your attention. But you don't interpret that as a crisis. You don't try to mask it with unhealthy happy habits. You just accept it as a reminder that you're mortal.

It's not easy to manage this brain we've inherited from our ancestors. It's the challenge that comes with the gift of life.

Keep in touch

Please sign up for my newsletter
Private Lives of Primates
at www.InnerMammalInstitute.org

And write to me if you discover something amazing about the inner mammal. I'm especially interested in how you explain it to your friends, family and coworkers.

Loretta@InnerMammalInstitute.org

Author's Note

My personal story is not the subject of this book, but I include it here because I always want to know the author's background when I read a book. I omit loved ones who are still alive, both for their privacy and because my circuits were built long before they came along. I am frank about those who have passed because it's relevant to my wiring. Like everyone, I built quirky circuits in youth. I've learned to survive with the circuits I have, and I've managed to build some new ones.

My quirky habit is holding my breath. I don't want to hold my breath, of course, so I sympathize with readers who have a habit they'd rather do without. I didn't realize I was holding my breath until I turned fifty. I knew something was wrong, but I didn't know what it was. I was always good at holding back my reactions to things, but I never thought of that as a problem. It was my best survival skill. My mother was violent and her favorite saying was, "Stop crying or I'll give you something to cry about." So I did. I've decided to relate these experiences because it can help people see the power of early experience instead of blaming individual outcomes on genes or "our society."

My story starts in Brooklyn in 1953. A month before I was born, I stopped moving. The umbilical cord had wrapped around my neck, I'm told. During the birth process, the cord tightened and I would have strangled to death, but, in my mother's words, "they pushed you back in until they could get a specialist to cut you out." I was born with red welts around my neck that lasted for three weeks. I imagine my mother fared badly as well.

According to my mother, I cried constantly for the first three months of my life. She told me how hard this was on her, but now I realize it was hard on me, too. I wonder if I was struggling to breathe, or if I was ever picked up.

My mother had a reason to react badly to the sound of crying. She was responsible for two younger siblings when she was just a child herself. My grandmother worked at a garment factory, and my mother had to feed the hungry mouths. She did the shopping and cooking and even the budgeting necessary to make their food last until the next payday. My mother had to focus on other people's needs without anyone focusing on her needs. I think bad feelings she had long buried were triggered by my tears. But she didn't know how her brain worked, so it seemed that I was causing her bad feelings.

My mother had a lot of bad experience stored in her brain. Her father was a violent predator. Once he tried to kill my grandmother with a cord around her neck. My mother had grown up with a lot of terror. She told me very little of it, but she's the only one of the four sisters who functioned in the world at all when they were adults.

When I was six months old, my mother's bad feelings escalated because she found herself pregnant again. "I cried and cried when I found out" she later told me. I felt bad for my brother when she said that. Then I realized that I experienced it, too. Of course, I feel bad for her. In fact, feeling bad for her was the core experience of my life.

During my brother's baptism party, I fell off a changing table and got a skull fracture. The doctors said nothing could be done except to keep me quiet. This was a huge burden on my mother, she told me, because I had just learned to walk and did not want to be penned up. The family worried that I would be brain-damaged until I was pronounced normal when I started kindergarten.

I don't remember any of this. My memory begins with my mother beating me. I don't know how old I was, but I remember my brother and I running from her and me falling on top of him when my mother started whacking me. I remember saying, "I'm sorry, I'm sorry, I'm sorry" without knowing what I was sorry for. I was always trying desperately to calm her.

My father was as scared of my mother as I was. He dealt with it by ignoring her, so that's what I learned to do. I avoided making eye contact with her the way New York subway riders used to avoid eye contact for fear of attracting predators. Of course, I didn't know I was doing this. I thought I was being good by staying out of the way. When I grew up, I was horrified to learn that people think badly of you if you don't make eye contact.

I had little opportunity to interact with other kids when I was young. I think I was afraid to play with my brother because the noise upset my mother. When I played baseball on the street with the neighborhood kids, the conflicts over points made me very anxious. They were just verbal arguments– nothing ominous, but I was triggered in a way I didn't understand.

My elementary school was full of kids bussed in from the nice part of town that hadn't gotten its own school yet. I was tracked into accelerated classes where almost all of the kids were

Jewish. "The Jews won't like you," my mother told me. When they invited me to their homes, she complained about having to drive me. When I got invited to their parties, my curfew was soon after the starting time. I didn't get invited very often. I didn't know why, but I knew I was treated better at school than I was at home.

My mother's schooling was undermined by moving eleven times when she was young. Her parents split up six times and got back together five times, and my grandmother insisted on moving each time to avoid the social stigma of having a man appear or disappear. They moved one subway stop east each time, making it from Brooklyn to Queens by the final split. At the time, when my mother was fourteen, my grandmother's income went up thanks to production for World War II.

My mother's older sister was schizophrenic. This diagnosis came when my aunt was forty-two and the passing of my grandmother forced her to interact with the world directly for the first time. While my grandmother was alive, my aunt often got into fights with people, but they went to the factory and home together each day. When my aunt had to live alone, she started calling the police and accused her landlady of breaking into her refrigerator and adding pepper to her carrots. The landlady got her evicted and my aunt lived on the subway until the police found her and she was finally institutionalized.

Once I had a therapist who said it's impossible for schizophrenia to be overlooked until you're forty-two years old. She obviously lived in a world where a delusional rager cannot just blend into the general craziness. I wish I lived in her world. I grew up in a world where accommodating crazy people was the norm. My mother dutifully chose her older sister as maid-of-honor at her wedding and as my godmother when I was born.

My mother did a lot of screaming when I was growing up. I stayed in my room reading as much as possible. In our tiny house, it sounded like an opera was blasting on the other side of the door. My whole room vibrated, but I was skilled at tuning it out unless the lyrics were about me. I was often the villain in my mother's opera. In her mind, I was abusing her. Now I know she was really mad at other people, but I didn't at the time. I tried to comfort her without success.

I felt like crying all the time when I was young, but I didn't. It would upset my mother and make me look dumb in front of other kids. Most important, it hurt. I remember waking up in the morning with terrible pain in my ribs from crying myself to sleep. I think I contracted my whole chest to stop the pain. Perhaps this caused the nervous ticks I had in elementary school. A chiropractor recently told me that some of my ribs are dislocated. But many decades went by before I had the leisure to acknowledge any of this.

When I was young, I was always reminded of how good I had it. When my mother was fourteen, she was invited to quit school and work in the factory like her older sister. After one day at a factory, my mother decided it was not for her. She got to stay in school and be the housekeeper in the afternoon. She became the first high school graduate in her family and took secretarial courses so she could work in an office. She lived with her family until a year after she married my father, since he was drafted into the military. By the time he came home, my mother had saved enough money for a down payment on a small house. And that is how I ended up in a "good" school district.

I did not have goals to speak of when I was young because my mother seemed to get mad when I showed interest in anything but her. But I always had good grades. It's easy to see why, since I was happy to have anything but "opera" to focus on, and I was scared to get caught doing something wrong. In school, I witnessed a world in which people didn't scream at each other. I didn't get much attention in school, but nothing bad happened either.

On the day I turned sixteen, I went looking for a part-time job. I was hired by a dry cleaners to work behind the counter for $1.60 an hour. I was fired in three weeks. People would show up the day before their wedding or bar mitzvah and their clothes would be missing. The evidence always pointed to me. It was humiliating, but I learned a valuable lesson. I hadn't been paying attention to detail because I thought it was a "dumb job." I learned that details matter, and looked for another job. By senior year in high school, I was a "paste-up artist" at the local *Pennysaver*. I earned two dollars an hour off-the-books for as many hours as I wanted to work.

I was rich.

And I got to keep the money instead of turning it over to support my family. I used it to plan my escape.

I wanted to go to a "sleep-away" college like the kids around me, but I was afraid that my mother would veto it if I acted like I wanted to leave her. Italians live under their parents' roof until they're married. So I played it cool on the subject of college. I poured my enthusiasm into the dream of taking myself on a Grand Tour of Europe.

The kids in my school always seemed to be going to Europe. Paris was the happiest place on earth, I'd learned from the French textbooks that had brightened my day for so many years. I found a study abroad trip that cost $1,000, and was happy to spend 500 hours at work to pay for it. The only obstacle was getting my mother's permission. For the first time, I was not going to take "no" for an answer. I begged relentlessly until she agreed. So while other kids were planning for proms and graduation parties, I was packing my hot pants (the 1971 fashion staple) and my *Petit Dictionnaire Larousse.*

As for college, things worked out as if I'd had a guardian angel. The guidance counselors called in each family during junior year to make plans. I was stunned to hear him tell my mother that I was near the top of my class and that I should apply to Cornell. I would never have guessed that my class rank was high since the smart kids didn't talk to me. I got mediocre grades in art, which is what interested me. Though I'd always had high grades and test scores, I never dared to think I was "doing well."

My mother was too intimidated to say "no" to the guidance counselor, and my father went along with her as usual. So it was a plan. I got admitted, I got scholarships, and I went from Paris to Cornell.

I was not a typical college kid. I felt like I was on easy street because I got to do homework without hearing my mother screaming in the background. I was in heaven because I got to choose my own meals and my own schedule without being heckled. When other students talked about how hard they had it, I didn't get it. I hated listening to their whining. I guess I wasn't a "good friend."

I was not even slightly tempted to follow the crowd. Of course, I wanted to be accepted like anyone else, but I could not imagine doing anything that risked landing me back where I came from. Probably I couldn't imagine being accepted either.

I loved psychology, economics, and sociology. Changing the world was the core topic of every course. Like any young person, I found that idea appealing. But it started to feel like every class was around the same thing– the terrible oppression we suffer at the hands of capitalists. I absorbed the message, though it didn't help me make sense of my experience. The dire warnings about "suburbia" and "consumerism" that were so popular in those days didn't ring true to me. I knew there were much worse things in life than living in the suburbs and watching deodorant commercials. Every teacher told me "our society is bad" in one way or another. It was like a club you could only join by hating yourself.

Despite my reservations about college, I had no where else to go. So I kept signing up for another tour of duty, getting a PhD and becoming a college professor.

I focused on Economic Development because it met the social expectation of "saving the world" while indulging my love of travel. I was still feeling guilty about not having saved my mother, so this was a good way to salvage my self-respect without going home.

I spent a year in Africa with United Nations Volunteers after my Master's Degree. That forced me to challenge the theoretical world view I'd learned in school. In my textbooks, Africans were always victims of Western oppression. But in my experience, African police stopped cars to get bribes, and African leaders stole foreign aid money. I saw how everyone looked the other way or invoked theories to excuse this behavior. I was not willing to invest my life in that habit. After all

I went through to escape from one bad system, I couldn't risk joining another.

When I came home, I appreciated "civilization" instead of just condemning it the way I had learned to in college. I understood how much it takes to have institutions that basically function. In college I'd learned to sneer at things that didn't work, but gradually I learned to notice what worked.

I stopped reading the news because it filtered out the good and magnified the bad. In the news, venting anger at leaders is glorified as the quintessential public service. But it's easy to see that people vent because it feels good, and recruit facts that fit. When I learned the word "nihilism," I was thrilled. The fact that the word existed proved I wasn't the only person who questioned this negativity, even when it was dressed up as a civic virtue.

My secret shame from the past is that I took jobs with great training programs, and then quit when the training was over. I did not intend to do that, but once I understood what these jobs involved, I couldn't make myself believe in them. I would never want me for an employee. My teachers taught me that management is evil, but I learned that employees are not necessarily good. My father ran a shop when I was young (a "pop" shop with no "mom") and he barely broke even. Though I was educated to believe that profit is evil, I came to understand that it's very hard to make a profit.

When I turned thirty, I was a wife, a mother, and a college professor. I forced myself to stick with this job, grateful that I had some control over my work. But in truth, I complained a lot. I always suspected my students were not doing the reading. It was not always clear that they knew how to read.

Other professors were quick to say it wasn't the students' fault. It was "our society's" fault. Once I had two kids of my own in school, the realities of human motivation hit me. My kids were not doing the reading, though they'd be defined as "privileged" by college professors. Once I saw my own kids suffering from "non-judgmental" low expectations, I opened my mind to other ways of thinking. I could not share this with my university colleagues. They clung to their low-expectation theories, and I noticed sadly that they either didn't have kids, or they had kids who didn't do the reading.

As the decades went by, I always found ways to travel and I always followed research in psychology.

My love of travel led me to study other cultures. I started with the idealized view that caring and sharing is the norm in other cultures, while "our society" has problems. But after spending a lot of time abroad and with students from other countries, I learned that humans have problems everywhere. Open acknowledgement of problems is not tolerated in many cultures. They don't report things to police and statisticians, and harsh reprisals often befall those who do. This makes it easy to think life is bad in open societies where problems are talked about.

I fell in love with psychology the first morning of my freshman year. I covered the walls of my dorm room with beautiful illustrations from *Psychology Today* magazine. I never considered a career in psychology because I knew I would drown if I swam in other people's pain. But I had a strong urge to understand human nature. For so much of my life, the facts of human behavior were unmentionables. Psychology seemed like a place where those facts could be brought to the light of day. As an amateur in the field (which means "lover," in Latin), I was able to delve into a wider range of psychological perspectives than I might have if it were my profession. No single theory was fully convincing to me, so I always kept looking.

I taught International Management for twenty years. Students from dozens of countries were in my classes. My MBA students were often mid-career professionals in arenas where bribes and kickbacks were expected. I wanted to teach my students how to refuse. It's a felony under US law to bribe for business in foreign countries. The law holds you guilty of bribery if you route your business through insider-middlemen who do nothing but pass along a "fee." Yet many countries refuse to do business with you unless you bow to such extortion. I did not want to tell my students to just "respect the culture," as foreign aid workers told me. I wanted my students to say "no." I couldn't find reading material to tell them that, so I wrote the book myself, *Greaseless: How to Thrive without Bribes in Developing Countries.*

As my fiftieth birthday approached, the nice people in Human Resources sent me an unsolicited message about my retirement benefits. I had never thought of retiring, but the idea started growing on me. Instead of doing the same thing forever, I decided to do something else while I still had the energy. My kids were grown, my body was aging, and I wanted to write and sell books.

As my commitments went down, my awareness of my breathing constriction went up. Possible solutions got my attention. I sampled a dozen different mind-body therapies, such as meditating, acupuncture, chiropractic, Rolfing, cranial-sacral therapy, talk therapy, eye movement therapy, NeuroLinguistic

Programming, Reiki, and my favorites, the Rosen method, yoga, qi gong, and many styles of massage. None produced instant miracles, but all felt great and taught me a lot. I learned from their similarities and from their differences. I used to think it was silly to fuss about the space between your vertebrae. Today, that space is one of my most valuable assets. When people tell me how awful the world is, I think their spine must be scrunched. But I don't say it.

While learning about my autonomic nervous system, I stumbled on the fact that animals have the same neurochemicals as humans. This was a revelation for me. It felt like the explanation of human nature I'd always been looking for. The neurochemicals that cause our ups and downs steer animals toward survival behaviors and away from survival threats. I was thrilled to have an explanation of real behavior instead of idealized notions of how people should be. I read everything I could find about the link between mammalian neurochemicals and behavior. I trained to be a docent at my local zoo (and persevered when the training was over!). I was surprised that our mammalian neurochemistry gets so little attention, so I decided to give it that attention myself. I wrote *I, Mammal: Why Your Brain Links Status and Happiness.* And that book led to this one.

Source Notes

The information in this book was synthesized from hundreds of sources. A recommended reading list on the mammal brain (as well as a movie list) is provided at my website: www.InnerMammalInstitute.org. (Select: Extras, I, Mammal.)

Synthesizing is a way of transcending the limits of individual sources. I encourage readers to synthesize information from a wide range of sources, with the following limitations in mind.

Pharmaceutical research

Medical research gets funded when it is linked to an explicit cure. Such research is not a complete picture of human emotion, and we should not expect it to be. Furthermore, big companies become targets of lawsuits. They must choose their research projects with such consequences in mind.

Academic research

University professors must generate data that passes "peer review" in order to survive. Academics know how their peers review things, and they know better than to risk their survival. For example, they need "good data" to avoid criticism, so social science research tends to focus on variables that are easily quantifiable, such as race, gender and income. As a result, we get a lot of with "information" that sifts human experience through a filter of race, gender and income. We take it as the complete truth because it's "statistically proven." Since "good data" on early childhood experience is not available, it is widely overlooked in the picture painted by academic research.

Self-reporting

Happiness research is often based on self-reporting. This introduces significant biases. In some cultures, you don't admit it if you're unhappy, especially to strangers with clipboards. You're expected to be content, so you find a way to do that. In other cultures, brooding unhappiness is respected as "deep," while happy people are dismissed as "complaisant" or "dull." Self-reported indicators of happiness are also easily biased by the wording of a question.

Therapeutics

Therapists don't want to scare people away. Anything deemed "off-putting" is likely to be left out of research that comes from the psychotherapy profession. Good intentions can create a customer-is-always right view of psychology, leading to unfortunate distortions. For example, abusive parents might resist therapy if they feel "blamed," so the therapeutic community dismisses abuse as the consequence of one injustice or another. This has value when it motivates parents to change. But it's harmful when it suggests that child abuse is a reasonable response to the frustrations of life. Humans have struggled to feed their families since the beginning of time, but the "therapeutic" perspective offers the enticing presumption that today's struggles are unprecedented. The non-judgmental view of child abuse may be "therapeutic" for the therapist in the moment he encounters the "client," but it is not necessarily best for the child and the society.

Contrarianism

Humans enjoy proving they're right and others are wrong. This impulse has motivated humans to search for the truth by disproving earlier truths. Over the millennia, contrarianism has improved our understanding of human behavior. But the joy of proving others wrong can also lead to misperceptions and distortions. For example, one popular strain of research purports to "prove" that humans are irrational using highly contrived scenarios. They offer subjects the chance to save five lives by taking one life. Most people think that's a good thing until the researchers suggest those five people be saved from an oncoming trolley car by pushing a fat man onto the tracks. Many respondents refuse. This study is widely cited as "proof" that we're irrational. That interpretation ignores the very rational inference that the trolley might not stop when the fat man is pushed at it, and the pusher could end up in jail for murder. Perhaps this contorted finding is accepted as "science" because it feels good to accuse the whole human race of irrationality.

Social engineering

It feels good to help others, so we like research that points the way to a "better world." But humans are more complicated than we expect, and formulas for fixing the world often have unintended side effects. For example, legalizing drugs can fix the world according to one strain of research, but such studies make simplifying assumptions and cannot possibly anticipate the full consequences of legalizing drugs. An engineer doesn't re-design a part until he knows how it fits into the whole.

Careerism

Every researcher knows which findings will win respect in their field and which will get them immediately shunned. Findings that fit current intellectual trends are eagerly reported in scholarly journals and the mass media. Findings that contradict the views of current opinion leaders often get buried in the researcher's desk because they can easily ruin the career of a "scientist." In every generation, new opinion leaders build careers by battling prevailing thought habits, only to impose new thought habits as rigidly as the old guard they so vehemently critique.

Ideology

Human beings see the world through the filter of their beliefs. Scientists are human, and have beliefs of their own. The scientific method elevates data from the biased perceptions of individuals. But when every study reported by a particular group of researchers just happens to reinforce their shared belief system, it makes me skeptical. For example, current research on happiness reinforces the Buddhist belief system, even though the researchers perceive themselves as practitioners of "hard science" rather than "religion." Similarly, research on animals reinforces the belief that kindness is the state of nature and unkindness is caused by "our society." I'm not against Buddhism or kindness, but I'm against the gross oversimplification of human nature that ideology can produce.

Decades of research have provided us with tremendous insight into human nature. However, distortions are likely at each moment in time because new ideas puff themselves up to gain acceptance. Advocates of new views strive to establish themselves by ridiculing and displacing representatives of other views. Decades pass before the merits of both views can be weighed outside the context of this mammalian dominance struggle. For example, Freudians ridiculed the "superstitious" thinking that came before them. Then behaviorists ridiculed the Freudians. Now genetics is popular and behaviorism is ridiculed. Each wave of insight makes a valuable contribution. But each wave tends to exaggerate its own contribution and understate the significance of prior insights. Each of us is free to synthesize research from many time periods instead of depending on what's popular at the moment. Interestingly, most of today's raging arguments were addressed a hundred years ago by William James's ground-breaking "Principles of Psychology." But James's positive contributions are mostly forgotten today, as people remember his misguided ideas about communicating with the dead. Every original thinker is right about some things and wrong about others, which prepares the way for the next swing of the pendulum. Each of us is free to synthesize our own insights instead of riding the latest swing.

Postcards from the Brain

Beautiful free downloads of these postcards are available at www.InnerMammalInstitute.org select: Extras, Meet Your Happy Chemicals

There is no free happy chemical in nature.

To get more, you have to do more.

meetyourhappychemicals.com

If it feels good,

it has
side effects.

meetyourhappychemicals.com

© 2012 L. Breuning

Your cortex and your limbic system are not on speaking terms.

When you talk to
yourself, it's all in
your cortex.

meetyourhappychemicals.com

© 2012 L. Breuning

No one can trigger your
happy circuits for you.

And you can't trigger
someone else's.

meetyourhappychemicals.com

© 2012 L. Breuning

There is no free love
in nature.

Sex has a preliminary
qualifying event
in every species.

meetyourhappychemicals.com

© 2012 L. Breuning

Your brain seeks status as if your life depended on it

because in the state of nature, it does.

meetyourhappychemicals.com

© 2012 L. Breuning

Your survival is threatened as long as you're alive.

Cortisol will always have a job.

meetyourhappychemicals.com

© 2012 L. Breuning

People are secretly respecting you behind your back

You may as well feel good about it.

meetyourhappychemicals.com

© 2012 L. Breuning

The brain is always trying to replace bad feelings with good feelings.

That "do something" feeling promotes survival, but it causes trouble, too.

meetyourhappychemicals.com

© 2012 L. Breuning

**My operating system
may be quirky**

but it has successfully
promoted survival for
200 million years.

meetyourhappychemicals.com

© 2012 L. Breuning

**If you believe "they" control
your happiness**

you don't learn to create
it in your brain.

meetyourhappychemicals.com

© 2012 L. Breuning

Loretta Graziano Breuning

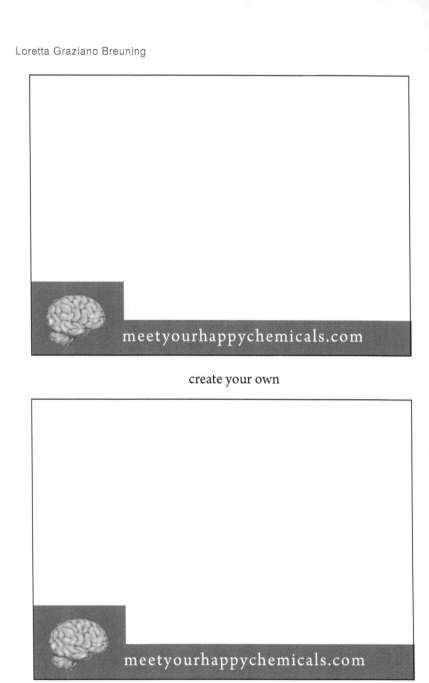

create your own

Index

This book avoids many well-known concepts in psychology in order to focus on the mammalian neurochemistry behind the labels. The following terms are not included: addiction, altruism, depression, ethics, left-brain/right brain, friendship, genes, meditation, mental illness, parenting, pleasure, religion, self-esteem, stress, therapy, success.

42113537R00119

Made in the USA
Lexington, KY
08 June 2015